WHAT IF I HAD 26 HOURS A DAY

A New Approach to Time, Productivity and Possibility

Biswajeet Senapati
and
Dr. Sharda Acharya

Dedication

We would like to dedicate this book to the
following people:

Biswajeet & Sharda's parents

We are grateful for everything they've taught us and continue
to teach. This book is a reflection of them.

Smita

The reviewer of this book, Biswajeet's best half and best
friend. Without your help, support, and guidance this book
would not have been possible.

Amit and Arihant

Amit, Sharda's consort. You have always stood by
my side for whatever endeavours I have indulged into,
like a rock.

Arihant, Sharda's son. You have inspired throughout,
to keep the time and tell stories that matter.

Swati Swagatika Panda

The official proofreader of this book. Your inputs were truly
vital for the completion of the book. Thank You for doing
this selflessly and in such a short span of time.

Contents

Preface

Congratulations. You have chosen to read this book. What can you expect from a book like this? There are plenty of motivational books available which can change your life. Why should you read this book? This book is not just for motivation. This book doesn't talk about time management techniques. It's about developing the right attitude towards time management. It's about being cognizant of the fact that time is not only about spending, but you can also earn time. When we embarked on this shared journey with the common view that, a man is not rich only by wealth, a man is rich who has time + money. Hence, we realised the need to pen it down. If you have a lot of money, but your driver, your maid, your security guard are enjoying that while you are busy at increasing your wealth, that's pathetic. Remember that time is a limited resource and that how we use it directly impacts the quality of our lives. A right attitude towards time management involves being proactive rather than reactive, setting clear boundaries, and learning to say no to distractions or tasks that do not align with your dreams, goals and values. Take charge of your day, create more meaningful experiences, and find balance between work, rest, and personal growth. Use this book as a self-check list. We, the authors, Mr. Biswajeet Senapati and Dr. Sharda Acharya, each bring our own unique perspectives to the work, yet our collaboration was born out of a deep desire to address the problem of 'time nehi hai', something we both care about deeply.

Biswajeet Senapati being a motivational speaker, a freelance career counsellor, a brain coach, understands the value of images over text. That's why he emphasised on the use of many images in the book which can always be recollected easily. He is instrumental in shaping an ideal belief system about Time.

On the other hand, Sharda Acharya, a teacher by profession whose experience in balancing professional responsibilities with family and household duties, played a vital role in creating relatable experiences for many. Together, we worked to weave our individual strengths into a cohesive whole.

The inspiration for this book came from our shared experiences and the realization that everyone is sailing in the same boat in this century. We believe that 'Time' is an important conversation that needs to be had, and we hope this book offers valuable insights to those seeking to look at it with a new perspective.

Don't forget to share your feedback. Wish you all the success in life. Happy reading!

I Don't have Time - Breaking the Excuse Barrier

"Time is a created thing,
To say, "I don't have time is to say",
"I don't want to."
~Lao Tzu, Chinese philosopher

Once a friend said – "You know, mujhe marne tak ki fursat nahi hai" (I don't have time to even die). We are sure many of us at some point used this statement. And we find this popular among mothers, especially working mothers.

Here is a general conversation between two close buddies.

Mo - I am too busy. I don't get any time to watch even a one minute reel.

Jo - Really, do you think it's an achievement?

Mo - What do you mean?

Jo - I mean if you consider it an achievement, I wish you become 25 hours busy in a day.

Mo - Are you mocking me?

Jo - Not really, but the way you people say, I am very busy to attend a birthday or read a book, I feel you take pride in that.

Mo - But, seriously I don't get time dude.

Jo - So you agree that it's a problem?

Mo - Hmm, I really don't know.

Jo - There you go. If you don't know that it's a problem, then I don't think you are even looking for a solution to it.

Mo - Really Jo, I never thought about it.

Jo - I can understand Mo. It's not only about you, 99% of people don't ever think about it.

"The human mind is really amazing. It can make excuses for anything that we don't want to do and can very well convince us with proper logical reasoning why we can't or shouldn't do it."

Excuses are the narratives we create to justify, and it often arise as a defence mechanism. Here are some you might hear almost daily and maybe you make some of them in your daily life.

- I don't have enough time
- I'm not good enough
- I'm too tired
- This is not necessary

And the list can be long enough. The problem with excuses is that they tend to become a habit. When we allow ourselves to make excuses repeatedly, we reinforce a mindset of helplessness and passivity. Over the time, our mind starts believing that external factors or circumstances are to blame for our shortcomings.

A patient went to a doctor.

Patient - Dr. I have got high cholesterol.

Dr - Hmm, your report doesn't look good.

Patient - Is everything okay?

Dr - Yes, yes, don't worry. Take these medicines & regular exercise for 30 mins.

Patient - Yes, Dr. I should exercise, but the problem is I am the senior delivery manager of XYZ. I hardly get any time.

Dr - I can understand, see what best you can do for yourself. Next patient please.

After 6 months

Patient - Dr, I don't feel comfortable these days. My work is getting affected. Please do something.

Dr - Let me check your reports.

Patient - Is everything okay?

Dr - I am afraid, you don't have much time left.

Patient - What do you mean?

Dr - You just have 6-9 months left.

Patient - Are you serious? I have my daughter's marriage next year. My son is still in college. Can't you do something?

Dr - Not really, only you can do something.

Patient - Tell me, I can do anything for it.

Dr - Find just one hour for yourself every day.

Patient - Done deal. I can. Tell me what to do? Where should I come? How much money it would cost?

Dr - Nowhere. Just go to a park & exercise for 1 hour daily.

Patient - That's all and I will be fine?

Dr - But I am afraid, you can do that. Last time you said, you really don't get any time for yourself.

What do you think the patient would have done after that? Do you think he would ever brag about the fact that he doesn't get time? Do you think he could get one hour every day from his super busy schedule? This may look exaggerated, but hope the point is clear.

The Hidden Hours

Now we know that the real issue is not a lack of time but how we choose to allocate the time we have. Hidden hours are those moments in our daily routines that go unnoticed or underutilized. They are the gaps between scheduled activities, the pauses in our busy lives, or even the time spent waiting. These intervals, which might seem too brief to make a difference, can accumulate into significant blocks of time if recognized and harnessed effectively.

When Biswajeet wrote his first book, people started asking him - from where on earth do you get time for this? First book is always special. It took him more than a year to complete and publish his first book. But when people ask him, which time did he use to write the book, he generally couldn't answer. Because there was no particular time in a day, where he would sit down and start writing it. Being a software engineer, father to twin school going kids, you never get a fixed time in a day. Moreover, you don't get ideas every day at a specific time of the day. What he did was the best use of those hidden hours in a day. Here are some hidden hours which we found for ourselves almost every day to complete this book.

Biswajeet

- When I go to pick my kids from school, I generally go 10-15 minutes before to avoid the parking issues.

- I spend everyday morning to play some gully cricket with a bunch of my friends. When our team is batting, I would wait for my turn.

- Whenever I go to doctor, 99% time, I have to wait and sometimes the wait lasts for hours.

- When I commute to work. In a city like Bangalore, I feel this is not a hidden hour, this can be the most productive hour of the day.

- Gaps between day tasks – once we finish a meeting, we take a break. If you add up all those breaks in a day, it can be really substantial.

- The period before going to bed and after waking up. Neither we wake up at one go nor we fall asleep at one go.

Sharda

- When every working morning is compact with multiple tasks of getting the child ready for school, feeding the family, managing the school supplies and lunches, personal preparation, potential tantrums of the child and above all the emotional labour of offering reassurance, encouragement and positivity to my child while trying to maintain my own energy and mental wellbeing, I manage to reach the workplace at least 30 minutes ahead of the expected time of arrival.

- When he is kept engaged with tuitions or badminton, I steal this time to replenish myself with Yoga- the ultimate method of self-connection and resilience.

No doubt it's the same for most of us and maybe you would add few more to your hidden hour list. Generally, we don't notice these stints as we are habituated to while them away. And these days, the best use of these gap-fillers are Instagram videos, YouTube shorts, WhatsApp forwards etc. You may ask what we can do in such small-time gaps? Believe me, 70-80% of Biswajeet's first book was written in those small gaps. You don't need to write a book though, but at least you can read a book. Here are a bunch of things which can be done for which we complain – "I Don't have time for this/that".

1. Read a book or an article.

2. Relaxation - Practices like deep breathing or short meditative sessions can be effective even in brief periods.

3. Organize Your Workspace – It's never a one-day activity. And if you try to do that, it would be a mess on 90% of the days.

4. Review your to-do list, prioritize tasks, and set goals for the remainder of the day.

5. Play a game with your kid.

6. Engage in Conversations with your kid/family.

7.   Read/prepare a story for your kids' bedtime.

These are some of the suggestions which we try to achieve every day. Depending on your lifestyle, you can have many more things to do in these small-time gaps.

"Your success will be in direct proportion to how you spend your 'free' time."

~Mike Dunlap

Then the second book was published – "When your kids grow older than you". People are now convinced that Biswajeet doesn't have a full-time job. And that inspired both of us to write the third book on time management.

Breaking the Excuse Barrier

Breaking the excuse barrier is a transformative process that begins with self-awareness and ends with empowered action. How do you deal with it then?

1. Recognize the Excuse Trap

The first step in breaking the excuse barrier is recognizing when we are making excuses. It requires honest self-reflection and awareness. Often, we're not fully conscious of the excuses we create, which is why they persist. The excuses may be subtle—like delaying tasks until tomorrow or convincing ourselves that we'll never be able to succeed at something. Being aware of these excuses is essential, as it allows us to challenge them head-on.

2. Replace Excuses with Action

Once we've identified our excuses, the next step is to replace them with productive actions. This involves shifting our mindset from "I can't" to "I can." Instead of focusing on why something is difficult or why we're unable to complete a task, we need to focus on overcoming the obstacles and move forward.

Breaking down a large task into smaller, manageable steps is one effective way to combat the feeling of being overwhelmed. When we approach challenges in bite-sized pieces, we make the task seem less daunting and are more likely to take action.

3. Build Self-Discipline

Self-discipline plays a pivotal role in overcoming excuses. Developing the ability to follow through on commitments, even when it's difficult or uncomfortable, is essential for success. Self-discipline requires making the right choices consistently, even when it feels easier to procrastinate or make excuses. Strengthening self-discipline involves practicing delayed gratification—resisting the urge to indulge in immediate comforts in favour of long-term goals.

Excuses can be any time, any where

A few years ago, I worked as a marketing manager for an online learning platform. We were quite a diverse bunch from multiple countries, myself included. Once or twice a year, we would hire a student or graduate on a paid internship. This was usually a three- to six-month contract, but if the person proved themselves and we were able to financially, we could extend the contract or take them on full-time.

One day, I got back from holidays and my boss, the Head of Operations, and a colleague had done a few interviews for a junior marketing role. My boss liked one candidate and wanted me to do the second interview, as they would be reporting directly to me.

The candidate was in their early twenties, newly graduated but impressive, and she aced the interview. But there was something bothering me; I just couldn't put my finger on what. After much debate with my boss and the CEO of the company — neither of them felt the same which, I did — we decided to hire her for three months on a fixed-term contract and see how it goes.

The first few weeks were great. She got to work early, she completed all tasks assigned within the deadline, she used initiative, she got along with other colleagues, and so on.

Then, little things started happening — the red flags my instincts were screaming about. This is a condensed version of her first-month review meeting with my boss and me.

Me: "[Intern], you've been doing really well with all the tasks I've assigned to you. I'm very happy with your work so far."

Intern: "That's great, thanks."

Boss: "I've had great feedback from a few colleagues, as well, so well done. There are a few small issues we'd like to discuss with you, though. [My Name] has mentioned that you've been in after 9:00 am a few mornings this week. With your contract being quite clear on a 9:00 am start, is there something going on that you want to share?"

Intern: "Oh, well, it's only a few minutes past 9:00. I don't think it's that big a deal."

Me: "It's been anything from a few minutes after 9:00 am to almost 9:30 am one day. And when you do get in, you spend at least ten minutes switching your computer on, making a coffee, and chatting with people. If there's a valid reason for getting in late, I'm open to reviewing your start time."

Intern: "So, the truth is that I live with my sister, and when I started working here, she wasn't working, so I had the bathroom all to myself. Now she's started a new job and she's in our bathroom when I need to get in there every morning. That's why I'm late every day."

My boss and I just stared at her, not really believing what we were hearing.

Boss: "That is really something you need to sort out with your sister. It is not a company issue and not something we can accommodate to give you a later start. Maybe get up earlier?"

Intern: "Oh, okay, yeah. I hadn't thought of that."

Boss: "The other area of concern is the amount of time you spend on your cell phone during the day. We have no issue with taking a quick personal call outside of your breaks, but it's been brought to our attention that you are constantly doing this every day, throughout the day."

Intern: "I'm not sure who's told you that, because I only take personal calls during my breaks."

Boss: "The CEO brought it to my attention, and I've seen you myself."

[Intern] kept quiet, not knowing what to say to this.

Me: "The bottom line, [Intern], is that you're a good worker with potential. These are small issues that are easily fixable by you. Now that we've told you about them, you can work on fixing them before we meet for your next review in a month's time. To summarise, I'd recommend that you get into the office about ten to fifteen minutes before 9:00 am so you've got time to settle in before you start work. And limit the personal calls to break times only, unless there's an emergency. And lastly, if there's an issue, talk to me. Sound okay?"

Intern: "Absolutely. I can definitely fix those things. Thanks so much!"

She did not; it only got worse. By her second review meeting, it was most of the above conversation all over again. By the third, we told her we were not extending her contract.

Source: notalwaysright.com

"I don't have time is often a barrier to confronting our true priorities; breaking it reveals the choices we're really making."

Chapter 2

The Joyful Calendar - Attitude Towards Time Management

"Yesterday's the past,
tomorrow's the future,
but today is a gift.
That's why it's called the present."
~Bil Keane

Why should I read a book on time management?

You see, there are dozens of books on how to manage time. There are some really simple, implementable ideas already prescribed in those books. And a lot of people read those books as well, but still become busy in due course of time. We believe time management is not about learning techniques to manage time. Of course, the techniques are important, but actually it's the attitude that we carry towards time that decides how we manage time.

Have you noticed this in your day-to-day life?

If you fix a time of 8 PM for some party or get together, some people will arrive at 8:15 PM. Next time you fix the time at 8:15 PM, the same set of people would arrive at 8:30 PM. No points to guess what time they would come if you fixed the time at 8:30 PM. Do you really think it requires time management skills to reach a function on time? You may think - how does that matter even if I am a few minutes late to a party? At that moment, it really doesn't matter. But it creates its own little ripple effect. Unconsciously you are building an attitude which says - Hey, even if I am 10-15 minutes late, it's perfectly fine. Here are some of aftereffects of this negligible attitude.

- Do you have a team member who is always late to a meeting? (Even 2 minutes late is considered late.)

- Do you have a friend who always misses the movie trailer in a theatre?

- Do you have a team player who is always late to practice session?

- Do you know a doctor who is always late to his clinic?

    You may ask – Is it really that big deal? Let's see.

The Ripple effect

Every day Biswajeet drops his twin kids at school before 7:45 AM as the gate closes by 7:50 AM. Most of the time he reaches before time, so that he is relaxed while dropping them near the school gate. However, one or the other day he gets little late due to a variety of reasons rather excuses. Even you must have noticed this - during the last few minutes, there is a maximum rush at the school gate. You would find more than 90% of the same faces every day during those last few minutes.

Sharda works in an engineering institute where she often has to invigilate in the semester exams that involves ensuring fair, secure and disciplined conduct of the examinees, taking their attendance, enforcing exam rules, maintaining time, handling issues of suspicious behaviour and emergencies, collecting back the answer scripts, reporting incidents and many other unforeseen situations. With the exam bell striking at 9 am, the examinees are frisked and entered inside the hall 45 mins earlier. Sharda and her colleagues have the window of 30 mins (8:30 am – 9:00 am) to report at the exam office. Winding up the morning chaos back at home, she sometimes reaches 10 to 9. Oh my god! Isn't that too late to set up the examination room before the bell goes.

You may ask –

- What's the problem if the kid enters the gate on time?

- What's the need to reach 30 mins ahead of others?

- What's the point of going before time?

Here is the deal. You must have experienced this kind of situation at different times.

Biswajeet's kids' school is in a residential area. So, in the morning time, the security personnel become ultra-active to manage the traffic in front of the gate which is a single lane 30 ft road. They manage it beautifully by dividing that small road into two halves. One for bikes and other for the three and four wheelers. They even take the pain of opening the car doors and taking the kids safely towards the school gate so that no car halts on the road. Still, you will find some people breaking the rules and changing lanes which is a very common thing. Next time you face this situation, take a pause and notice your emotions as well as the people around you. When you have enough time for the gate closure and someone breaks the lane, you would react casually and may utter a few words for the rule breaker.

But think of this situation, you are in the car lane, only 2 minutes left for the gate closure, and you have 10 cars in front of you. Suddenly you see a car breaks the lane & moves ahead of you. At this point, your reaction would be completely different. Often, we forget that we are with our kids, and we burst out.

Sharda resides at a stone's throw from her workplace. If she starts 10 minutes earlier than her usual schedule, she would no more be noticed as the last entrant for the job. Else, the stress of being held up, is passed on to the child who returns after an exhaustive time at school.

Do you see the difference of five minutes? No, it doesn't stop here.

- First, you pass the hard feelings to your kids.

- Second, you start your day in a frustrating mood.

- Third, whenever you get a chance, you discuss the matter and spread the negativity even further.

Being late might seem like a small issue, but its effects can have its ripple effects affecting morale, productivity, and even relationships.

Do you really think it's worth five minutes of your time?

Have you ever missed a bus, train or flight?

Each one of us have missed one or the other and may be some might have missed many. Do you think it's always due to some external factors? There can be quite a few genuine reasons for missing a bus, train or flight, But we would attribute at least a strong 50 percent towards the ripple effect of how we generally deal with time. Most of the time people give excuses or blame others.

- I was late because of him or her.

- I was caught up with something and didn't realize how late it was.

- The alarm didn't go off or was set incorrectly.

- There was huge traffic near the bus stop or station.

- My phone battery ran out and I could not follow my schedules.

- The travel app or website caused confusion about departure times or re-scheduling.

- I got the departure time wrong or confused AM/PM times.

- I just couldn't get up on time.

While these excuses might be the real reason behind missing the bus or train, it's often clear that the core issue is a lack of urgency or time management.

Rome was not built in a day neither your attitude

Biswajeet's wife usually complains – you always reach the venue before everyone and make us wait for others to come.

Wearing the seat belt is an attitude. A friend asked - it's just the next lane, hundred meters away, what's the point of wearing the seat belt. You can't even drive beyond 20 in this lane.

When you commit someone that you will be there for any occasion, make sure you meet it. And if you can't make it, don't give false promises. You can always say – "I will definitely try". People should brand you – there you see "the man or woman of words".

Why is it so important to build the attitude?

Drop by drop turns into an ocean. Wearing the seat belt when it's not required trains your subconscious mind to wear it when it's urgent and you would forget. Reaching a venue on time makes you feel punctual, and you always take pride on that. When people say you are a man or woman of words – imagine what kind of self-image you carry with you. And when you build the right attitude towards time, you really don't need to manage it. Just the way you drive the car or bike without thinking about when to apply the brakes, when to press the clutch, your mind would be automatically trained to manage time effectively and you would just have enough time to do all the required tasks in your day. When you approach tasks with a positive outlook, you're more likely to stay committed, and overcome distractions, leading to higher productivity in a lesser time. Building the right attitude towards time helps you appreciate the present. Rather than constantly worrying about the future or reflecting on the past, you learn to value the present moment, enjoy the process of living, and engage fully in your current experiences. The right attitude towards time allows you to make the most of every moment, reduces stress, increases productivity, fosters growth, and leads to a more fulfilling life.

"It's not about whether it's necessary or not,
it's about building that attitude which would work when
it's required the most."

You see attitude is one of the most important factors that not only helps in time management, but it can shape our lives in the long run. Building a positive attitude towards time management is a gradual process. Here are some tips to build the right attitude towards time over a period of time.

1. Recognize the Importance of Time

2. Shift from Procrastination to Proactivity

3. Develop Self-Discipline and Consistency

4. Set Clear and Realistic Goals

5. Eliminate Distractions and Focus on Priorities

6. Practice Flexibility and Adaptability

7. Learn from Mistakes

8. Stay Committed

9. Celebrate Progress

"A joyful calendar reflects a joyful life; when your attitude towards time management is rooted in purpose and passion, every moment becomes a celebration."

Chapter 3

Time Well Spent is Time Well Managed: I Don't Get Time for My Family

"At the end of your life, you will never regret not having passed one more test, not winning one more verdict, or not closing one more deal. You will regret time not spent with a husband, a friend, a child, a parent."
~Barbara Bush

I don't get time for my family

Do you know what is the biggest regret people have on their deathbed? Most of us must have read about this survey. At the death bed, people were asked, what could have they done differently if they were allowed to grow up again?

According to end-of-life care workers and medics, the number one regret is as follows:

"I wish I hadn't worked so hard and made more time to spend with my family and to enjoy myself more outside work."

Jo: I really don't get time for my family.

Mo: Why?

Jo: See, when I get up in the morning, my kids are gone to school. By the time I come back, they fall asleep.

Mo: Is it an everyday affair?

Jo: Almost every day.

Mo: Then your job is very demanding.

Jo: No, not really.

Mo: Then, why do you come so late?

Jo: I work overtime/ I earn a part time income/ I run a part time business/ I do tuition after job/ I run a private clinic in the evening etc.

Mo: Oh, but why are you working so hard?

Jo: Obviously, to earn more, to make life comfortable.

Mo: And all this for whom?

Jo: What an absurd question, for my family, for their future.

Mo: And at the cost of what?

Jo remained silent.

Mo: At the cost of family time, isn't it?

What do kids want?

Jo took his two young kids to a nearby fair one day. The fair was full of new toys, swings, tasty food and everything that can amaze any kid. As soon as they entered the fair, both the kids jumped with excitement and wanted to buy everything that caught their eyes. Jo carefully bought a few toys of kids' choice, let them enjoy the swings.

Suddenly Jo got a call from his boss and while talking over the phone he went a little far away where kids couldn't sight him. The kids searched for Jo for some time and after that they started becoming nervous. Soon they realised they can't find Jo. In a fraction of moment, the toys became boring, the swings became worthless, and the kids started crying. After some time, Jo was back in their sight. They threw all their toys and ran towards Jo. You might think, this is an example of young kids who don't realise the value of money. But if you can think of – that is exactly the time kids want more time from us, and we enjoy their company. The logical mind may say – once they grow up, they would not remember how much time I spent with them, all they would remember is what expensive gift I give him/her on 18th birthday. Now the question is – do you want your kid to enjoy your gift or enjoy your time & company. This may sound a little harsh, but more than the kids, we want to make our life comfortable, and we get an excuse in the form of our kids to earn more. We will discuss more about balancing hours and dollars but think about this harsh reality of our life.

Jo And the Fisherman

Once in a small village Jo was going around on his mini vacation. Suddenly his eyes caught a local fisherman who was about to go home after filling his basket with some quality fishes. He complimented the fisherman on the quality of his catch.

Jo - "How long did it take you to get all those fish?"

Fisherman - "An hour or two."

Jo - "Then why didn't you stay out longer to catch more?"

Fisherman – This much is sufficient to meet me and my family today.

Jo - "But what do you do with the rest of your time?"

Fisherman - I sleep late, fish a little, play with my children, and take a nap with my wife. In the evening, I go to the village to see my friends, dance a little, play the guitar, and sing songs. I have a full life."

Jo - "Well I have an MBA from IIM and I am sure I can help you for a better life. You should start by fishing longer every day. You'll catch extra fish that you can sell. With the revenue, you can buy a bigger boat. With the extra money you can buy a second boat and a third one, and so on, until you have an entire fleet of trawlers. Instead of selling your fish to a middleman, you can then negotiate directly with the processing plants and maybe even open your own plant. You can ship fish to markets all around the world. In time, you can then move to New York City to build your own enterprise."

Fisherman - "Wow, sounds like a plan. How long would that take?"

Jo - "Fifteen, may be twenty years"

Fisherman - "And after that?"

Jo - "When your business gets really big, you can sell stock and make millions!"

Fisherman - "Millions? Really? And after that?"

Jo - "After that, you'll be able to retire, live in a small village near the coast, sleep late, play with your grandchildren, catch a few fish, take a nap with your wife, and spend your evenings singing, dancing, and playing the guitar with your friends."

Fisherman – "And what do you think I am doing now?"

Without waiting for a reply, the fisherman left.

"Do you think it was worth spending those 15-20 years to get something what you can get right now?"

Best time to spend with family

During the growing age of our kids, most of the time, the father spends more time at work than with kids. We always have a logical reasoning that we are earning money which is really important for their education, their needs. We always feel that kids will be happier when they material demands are fulfilled, and we compromise their time with money. Nothing wrong in that. It's not that, we should not earn, but as a parent we can be smart and spend quality time with kids.

"Quality time always supersedes quantity time".

Do you know when is the best time to spend quality time with kids? Here are some simple ways to achieve the balance.

1. Get up 15 minutes early

Get up at least 15 mins early than you usually do. Best thing to start the day is with kids. Spend those extra 15 mins to wake them up. Cuddle them, hug them, talk to them, create some excitement. As they say - Morning shows the day, the first 15 mins can be a deciding factor for you and your kids' whole day.

2. Pick/drop your kid

If your kid is going to school, pick/drop them from/to school. The school may be 5 minutes away, may be 15 or 30 minutes away or even more. That is one of the best times to spend with your kids. While they are going to school in the morning, they are fresh and whatever conversation happens, would last for the day. When they are coming back from school, they have a lot of things to share, but once they reach home, they become busy with mobile/TV/food etc.

3. The family that eats together, stays together.

Our body is built from the food that we take. Each cell is a product of the food that we intake. Imagine all the members of the family building their cells together, obviously one of the best times to spend together. Of course, needless to say, no technical gadgets during food. No mobile, no television, no other distraction. Feel like you are building a family together.

4. The family that prays together, stays together forever.

If you have a spiritual bent of mind and you offer prayers every day, make it a habit to do with your kids. Believe it or not, that's the highest level of connection that you can build in the shortest possible time.

5. Read a book together.

Fix a time, just for 5 minutes is enough, 15-30 minutes is ideal though. But we are talking about busy me, so even 5 minutes will do. Everyday spend that time with your kids' reading any book that you love. Fix that time every day. Why book – It has double benefit. You can choose some other exciting activities as well as per your and your family's preference.

6. Sleep together

If your kids are young, in most cases, if they are less than 10-12 years, sleep together. Hug them, cuddle them, talk to them, practice some common dialogue to utter before you all go to sleep together. For example - Thank you God for a lovely day today. Good night. I have personally developed this habit so much that even when I am touring and not at home, before going to bed, my kids would call me and say good night. Try it, it's really worth of your busy schedule.

7. Go out together

If possible and feasible, go out on a small trip once in a month or in a quarter. Go out to a park or a shopping mall or a movie together once a week. Most of the time we wait for a big annual trip, but we forget that, the trip lasts only a week or so, and the memories of it may last for few weeks or months. Never lose out on small moments which can create lasting memories.

These small moments last long and it creates a satisfying emotion within you. You no longer feel that you don't have time for your family. These small changes create a ripple effect in your daily, weekly, monthly schedules. Spending quality time with family is crucial because it enhances emotional well-being, strengthens relationships, fosters personal development and creates lasting memories. These benefits contribute not only to individual happiness but also to a more supportive and resilient family dynamic. When you feel satisfied about the most important part of your life, i.e. family, you get the confidence that you can manage the whole world.

"Time well spent is a reflection of priorities well managed; if family feels neglected, it's not a lack of time but a misalignment of what truly matters."

Chapter 4

Busy by Choice: The Psychology of Excuses in Time Management

"Don't get so busy making a living that
you forget to make a life."
~Dolly Parton

Why is it, that everyone is so busy?

Have you ever carefully seen a mouse? Did you ever see it still? I feel it's the busiest creature on this planet. **But busy for what?** God created human beings as the most precious creature with the most powerful engine called "Intelligence". Should we also behave like a mouse? Sometimes, even God would be amazed to see humans on earth running for the basic things in life. Can we be humans?

It's a concerning pattern. People rush around like busy ants, completing their daily tasks, but perhaps not truly making progress or finding the happiness they expected. Many of us settle for a less-than-fulfilling "present," believing that if we just keep working hard and staying busy, we'll eventually reach a future where everything falls into place—a place where life is easier, and we can finally slow down and enjoy it. But to be frank, we all know at the bottom of our hearts that we are fooling ourselves.

Here is a snippet of Biswajeet's experience at work

When I confronted my lead

My first job was with an Indian MNC where I worked for couple of years. Here is an incident from that. I was a fresher and like many others full of attitude. But one thing which was always clear in my mind from the beginning of my career was to keep my evenings always free. Even after 20 years in the corporate world, I try my level best to have my evenings free no matter what. The company where I worked had the culture of clocking daily hours – they counted first in last out and the time in office should be at least 9+ hours. Being in Bangalore if you start your regular day at 9AM and spend 9 hours in office as per the company policy, you would reach back home not before 8 PM provided you are lucky. So, I always planned my day early. I remember in my development centre I used to be the first person to enter and mostly the first person to log out. At times, I would enter the office as early as 6 AM in the morning so that I can log out early and enjoy my evenings with my friends. I don't say, it's possible for everyone. I was a fresher with no one back at home, so I took advantage of that to the most. Now I am a father to twin kids, hold a responsible position in another MNC, but that habit of wrapping up early still holds good for me.

One morning, I reached little early at around 6:15 AM in the morning. Generally, when I enter the development centre the automatic sensor switch would get on and I loved that experience. As I walk down towards my cubicle, the lights would switch on with my passing footsteps. That day when I swiped in and entered the development centre, the switches were on already. I was surprised who had the guts to be in the office before me that to on a winter morning. Then my guess was right. It was one of the leads from another project who was very hard working. Her daily log out time would be usually 9PM at night. I slowly walked up to her.

Me: What are you up to? So early in the office?

Rachi: I was here the whole night.

Me: Where is your team?

Rachi: I asked everyone to leave.

(I was amazed by her. She looked tired after the sleepless night and was still working.)

Me: Coming for some coffee?

Rachi: Oh yeah, badly need one.

(And we both walked towards the canteen.)

Me: I know you are a workaholic, but whole night, what happened?

Rachi: There was a release last night, and something broke at the last minute.

Me: So what?

Rachi: What do you mean? We had to release that at any cost.

Me: Ok, calm down, I understand the pressure. But were you able to release that?

Rachi: No, whole team stayed late, but we couldn't figure out.

Me: And you stayed back taking the responsibility on your shoulder.

Rachi: Of course, I am the lead, I am accountable.

Me: So, is it fixed now?

Rachi: Not yet, still unable to find out the root cause.

Me: So when will you release it then?

Rachi: I am trying my best to make it today.

Me: So, it's ok if it gets delayed by a day?

Rachi: We don't have a choice.

Me: Exactly, do you think the earth would fall if this release got delayed by a day or two.

Rachi: You won't understand that as you are a fresher.

Me: In that case Rachi, I would not like to understand ever. I don't say we should not try. You tried your level best, but still it's delayed by a day. So where do you put a stop to it?

(She kept silent while sipping the hot coffee and our conversation ended there.)

One month later, while I was running out of office to catch the first bus, I saw one known face in the lift. Yes, it was Rachi. Again, she surprised me.

Me: What am I seeing today? Arc you alright?

(Rachi just smiled.)

Me: How come leaving so early today?

Rachi: Trying to make it a habit to come early and go early.

Me: Wow, incredible.

Rachi: Yeah, someone taught me, nothing is urgent in life.

I just smiled and we both left. I felt really good that I could mark my point to someone who was elder, experienced and wiser than me. Today, I have grown in my career, whenever I face such a situation, I fondly remember that incident which happened randomly one day.

*"Nothing in life except medical emergencies can
be urgent, unless you make it."*

This one is yet another chapter from Biswajeet's memory lane

Do you think technology is saving time for us?

I love to give career counselling to teenagers in my family and relatives. Sometimes I help with their studies as well. One day, I visited one of my close relatives after quite some years. The little toddler had grown up to a lad by then. The outdated parents had upgraded themselves to use mobile, Facebook, WhatsApp, Instagram etc. They welcomed me to their house. After our regular talk, like many other parents, they started complaining about the same problem - mobile over usage by their kid. While mother was complaining, father was busy checking his WhatsApp messages. I didn't reply anything to the problem immediately. I spent couple of hours in their house and the father hardly talked to me for few minutes. When I enquired if he was busy with some important mails at work, I realised that he had been playing a game all this while. Finally, while leaving when they asked me for a solution, I politely said - "Can you stop using your mobile when you are at home except for important calls"? And without waiting for an answer, I left. They were expecting me to advise the kid, explain the effects of mobile radiation etc.

Do you agree with what I said?

And here goes Sharda's story

Did you prioritize your goal?

When it comes to meeting deadlines at office, be it evaluating answer scripts, uploading sessional marks in the central portal, covering syllabus before the semester exams or submitting papers and abstracts for research journals, my priority has always been my ten-year-old son and things related to him. No compromise on spending quality time with him as I would never want him to feel deprived only because I am a working mother. Holistic development and wellbeing of my son is my greatest priority. It's a real time unplugging that needs right direction and pause. So here goes my strategy.

1. I recognize that one can't do everything at the highest level, and it's okay to be average in the areas that don't align with our core strengths or passions. By choosing to be average I reduce the risk of overextending myself, allowing myself to pour more energy into areas which align with my long-term goals. Hence, I never ran the race of rats and most of the times, avoid burnouts. But of course, some milestones need to be achieved even if it needs the midnight oil to be burnt because one needs to be visible in the market.

2. Some tasks that do not need top-tier performance might be outsourced. For example, a culinary and a domestic help. Panicking clouds judgement. So, I generally tend to be level-headed in situations where the emotions need control and clarity rather than fear, stress and anxiety. Gradually we realise that most challenges are temporary and manageable.

Mental health should be strengthened by practising meditation. A regular 108 times 'Om Namah Shivay' chanting with the water manifestation technique for good health, peace and prosperity is good to save you from all pitfalls of life. Do it with mindfulness to believe it!

Smart phones making us dumb?

Technology instead of being a boon, slowly becoming a time killer for most of us. Knowingly or unknowingly, we tend to spend a good amount of time on mobile these days.

With over 881.25 million internet users and a 71% smartphone penetration rate, India stands as one of the world's largest and fastest-growing markets for mobile technology. A shocking revelation by InMobi study says that -

Indians surpass the global average spend over 4 hours on smartphones daily.

You may think - what is the connection of being busy with smart phone usage. But ask yourself -

"Do you think all those hours can be utilised constructively if we had no smart phones?"

Here are few simple things you can try to feel little less busy in your everyday life.

1. Food without mobile or laptop

Make it a thumb rule, no mobile during food. These days, even small kids are not eating without a mobile. And we put the logic that he/she won't eat without YouTube. Really? Who has made that norm? Was he or she born with the mobile? The point here is - Are we so busy that we can't even have food without a mobile?

2. Do not check office stuff in mobile

Smart phones have really made our life smart and convenient. To some extent, it has made our life dumb as well. Many people tend to check their office mails/chats in mobile. Nothing wrong in doing that. But we become so habituated that we tend to check before and after office hours. It's okay to check when there is a need or ask, but do not make it a habit to check office stuff after office hours.

I used to get up in the morning and like many others, I used to check my WhatsApp messages and then straight to office mails and messages. Slowly I realised, I am getting occupied with office work in mind much before my working hours and that's purely a personal choice, no one asked me to do that.

So, a strict NO to office stuff before office hours.

3. Take breaks

Have you heard this - I was so busy today that I didn't even get time to have my lunch. Or this – I was so occupied today that I forgot my kid's annual function. This is what happens when we force our brain to work continuously without taking any breaks. No matter what, ensure to take a break after every 45 mins to 1 hour. The break need not a long one, a small relaxation, a cup of coffee is enough to rejuvenate your brain.

NOTE: Do not take the sip of coffee while you are still working.

4. Meditation

It has nothing to do with achieving spiritual heights. Just like our physical body, our mind needs rest as well as exercise. We have become smart to know that physical exercise is necessary, but we forget that our mind works more than the body. We all agree that to work smart; to use time effectively, we need a sharp, focussed and innovative mind.

But practically we don't do anything about it. Meditation is one of the best ways to achieve that. You can find your own ways to exercise your brain.

5. Spend time with kids and old

Kids have the best power to rejuvenate us and with old we get wisdom. No matter how busy we are, this time is the most important and believe once we do that regularly, we feel accomplished. If you don't have young kids or old parents at home, go to a orphanage and old age home.

6. Spend time with animals

If you are a pet lover and have a pet at home, nothing like it. Unknowingly, you are making the best use of your time. If you don't realise this, after a hectic day or a hot argument, go and sit near an aquarium, you would feel it. You need not pet an animal at home, just observe the street animals, the birds on the tree, that is sufficient to relax your brain. Believe me, those 5-10 minutes are worth spending every day.

7. Play some sports

You can go to a gym, walk few miles, do cycling, but nothing can match the time spent in a sports activity. I would rather play a game for 15 mins than walk on a trade mill for an hour.

8. Focus on one thing at a time

The problem is not less time, but the inefficient usage of available time. When we try to do multiple things together, we have to do a lot of context-switching. That way we kill one thought and create another. When we try to shift back to the previous task, we need to revive back the old thought process. This is exactly what kills our productivity and hence, time.

9. Spend time with Nature

Spending time with nature offers numerous benefits, including improved mental and physical health, reduced stress, increased creativity, and a deeper connection to the environment. Whether it's a short walk in the park or a weekend getaway to the mountains, nature has a powerful way of refreshing, rejuvenating, and restoring balance in our lives.

"Work while you work. Play while you play."

The reason behind spending time in all of the above is to make ourselves feel accomplished. And I always say - a feeling of accomplishment can work wonders in our life. When you are able to spend these small moments, you start feeling you can manage time well. And as the theme of this book goes, it's all about our feeling, building our attitude towards time.

Next time, when you get super busy, please ask yourself –

- Where is it leading me?
- Is my life heading in the right direction?
- Am I even aware of where my life is heading?
- Do I really need to be as busy as I am?

Retrospect - Could it be that your constant busyness is a way of avoiding deeper issues in your life? Take a moment to pause and reflect on how you're living. Consider whether changes could be made to bring more peace and contentment. Remember, being busy doesn't necessarily mean you're successful or happier—in fact, in most of the cases it might be just the opposite.

"Being busy is often a choice, not a constraint;
it's the psychology of excuses that masks
our true priorities."

Time Follows Priority - It's about Priority, Not Time Management

"Time is like massive block of marble—solid and unchanging. How we shape it depends on our priorities."
~Unknown

Let's make this thing clear in our mind. When we say, we don't have time for something, that clearly states, that something is not a priority for us at that point of time.

Story of a Common Man

Years ago, when Jo was just starting his career, he was faced with a crossroads. He had just begun working as an assistant at a prestigious firm and was eager to prove himself. At the same time, his family needed his support - his younger sister was getting married, and his parents needed help around their house. And on top of that, Jo had personal goals, to finish writing a book he'd been working on for years.

Overwhelmed by everything, he attempted to tackle each task in the order they came to him. At work, he stayed late, hoping to impress his boss, but ended up missing his sister's engagement party. When his parents asked for help, he promised to assist after work, but often found himself too exhausted. Meanwhile, his book remained incomplete, gathering dust in the corner of his room.

One particularly chaotic evening, Jo found himself buried under paperwork and yet unable to focus. His phone rang - it was his mother, asking him to attend a family gathering. He glanced at his watch, realizing that his writing deadline was just a few days away. It was then he had a revelation, he was trying to please everyone and spread himself too thin, but in doing so, nothing was getting the attention it deserved.

That night, Jo sat down with a pen and paper, creating a list of all his responsibilities.

<u>For the first time - He asked himself, "What truly matters to me right now?"</u>

When was the last you asked this question to yourself? I would recommend, we all should ask ourselves this question more often. Generally, as a thumb rule, we all assume during the middle phase of our life, money is the most important thing, and we spend as much time as possible on earning as much money as possible. But then, at the fag end of our life, we realise, we spent the golden period of our life in earning only one aspect of our life, we forgot the other very important aspect, i.e. TIME.

The famous story of the Woman and the Parrot

The story is told of a woman who bought a parrot to keep her company, but she returned it the next day. "This bird doesn't talk," she told the owner.

" Does he have a mirror in his cage? "He asked. "Parrots love mirrors. They see their reflection and start conversation.

The woman bought a mirror and left. The next day she returned; the bird still wasn't talking.

"How about a ladder? Parrots love ladders. The happy parrot is a talkative parrot.

The woman bought a ladder and left. But the next day, she was back.

"Does your parrot have a swing? No? Well, that's the problem. Once he starts swinging, he'll talk up a storm.

The woman reluctantly bought a swing and left.

When she walked into the store the next day, her countenance had changed.

"The parrot died," she said.

The pet store owner was shocked.

"I'm so sorry. Tell me, did he ever say anything?" he asked.

"Yes, right before it died," the woman replied.

"In a weak voice, it asked me, 'Don't they sell any food at that pet store?'"

Sometimes we forget what's really important in life. We get so caught up in so many things that are good while neglecting the things that are truly necessary and deserve our time. Take a moment to do a "priority check" and strive for what is most important today.

A sneak peek at Biswajeet's closet

What is important?

I think each one of us must have faced this situation in life. Last month, on one particular day, I had three invitations to attend different functions. One was my close friend's sister's marriage, other was my cousin son's first birthday and third one was my kids' friend's birthday. Can you guess which one I attended? Well, I attended two of them, though it was not easy to make time for two of the occasions on a working day. Now, it's not important which are the two I went to, but the point to note here is that how did I select the two. Do you think it was based on the time I had on that given day? Not really, it's the one or two which I choose to be the priority ones. And if all three were of same priority, I am sure I would have found some ways to attend all three. I am sure, you might have done the similar things quite a few times in your life.

Take this example – consider the difference between spending an evening working late at the office versus spending that same time with family or friends. Both choices involve the allocation of time, but the impact of each decision is vastly different. The first choice may seem like the responsible or productive thing to do, but over time, constant prioritization of work can lead to burnout or strained relationships. The second choice may feel like a more leisurely option, but it could be a reminder that nurturing relationships and connecting with loved ones is just as important, if not more so, than meeting deadlines.

What did Gandhi do when British authorities gave him 30 minutes?

When the British authorities came to arrest Gandhi on August 9, 1942, they gave him a half-hour notice to prepare himself. This gesture was a formality, allowing him a brief period to gather his thoughts and make final preparations. Gandhi, ever composed and serene, used this time to reflect and say farewell to his associates.

During those 30 minutes, Gandhi remained calm and took the opportunity to address his followers. He used the time to reiterate his commitment to the cause of independence and to offer his final thoughts and encouragement. He knew the importance of time, not only those 30 minutes, but there are number of examples of his disciplinary actions. He was clear on his goals and priority. So, even 30 minutes before going to jail, he was able to make the best use of that time.

"If we are clear on our priorities, we can always make the best use of our time."

How to choose the highest priority?

Generally, we get confused on prioritising the daily tasks. Big decisions are easy to make, but it's the daily chores which kills most of the time. To achieve true success and fulfilment, prioritizing meaningful activities in life is of utmost importance. Prioritization involves identifying what truly matters and dedicating one's energy to these key areas, rather than getting caught up in trivial or superficial concerns. Prioritizing daily tasks effectively is key to managing your time and achieving your goals. I can always have a long-term goal, dream or vision, but today matters. If I cannot manage today properly, chances are, I won't be able to manage tomorrow and day after. You can find these simple ways to put a check on your daily chores.

1. List Your Tasks

Listing your tasks daily is a highly effective way to stay organized and focused throughout the day. By writing down the tasks you need to accomplish, you can clearly prioritize what's most important and break down larger projects into manageable steps. A daily to-do list helps reduce the overwhelming feeling of forgetting something and allows you to track progress as you check off completed tasks.

2. Identify Urgent vs. Important

Urgent tasks are those that require immediate attention, often with deadlines or external pressure, while important tasks contribute to long-term goals and personal growth but may not need to be completed right away. It's crucial to differentiate between the two because focusing only on urgent tasks can lead to constant firefighting, leaving important but less time-sensitive work neglected.

3. Set Clear Goals everyday

By defining specific, measurable, and achievable goals, you create a roadmap that guides your actions and decisions throughout the day. Clear goals help you prioritize your tasks, ensuring that you dedicate time and energy to what truly matters. They also provide a sense of direction, reducing distractions

4. Estimate Time and Effort

By evaluating how long each task will take and the level of effort required, you can better organize your day and avoid overloading yourself. This process encourages you to break tasks into smaller, more manageable steps, making it easier to allocate appropriate time blocks. It also allows you to recognize tasks that might require more focus or energy, enabling you to prioritize them accordingly.

5. Create a Schedule

By mapping out specific time slots for each task, you can establish a clear structure for your day, helping you stay focused and productive. A well-designed schedule allows you to prioritize high-value activities, allocate enough time for breaks, and avoid overloading yourself with too many tasks at once. It also provides flexibility, as you can adjust time blocks based on unforeseen changes or tasks that take longer than expected.

6. Review and Adjust

At the end of each day, take a moment to evaluate what you've accomplished and identify any tasks that were left incomplete or took longer than expected. This reflection helps you understand where your time was well-spent and where adjustments are needed. It also allows you to fine-tune your approach for the next day by reallocating time for tasks that need more attention or shifting priorities based on emerging demands.

Eisenhower Matrix

One of our favourite tools to prioritise things is using the Eisenhower Matrix. The Eisenhower Matrix is especially useful because, in requiring you to prioritize tasks by urgency and importance, it helps you figure out what you can delegate (or even not do at all) so that you can instead focus on the things that truly deserve your time and effort.

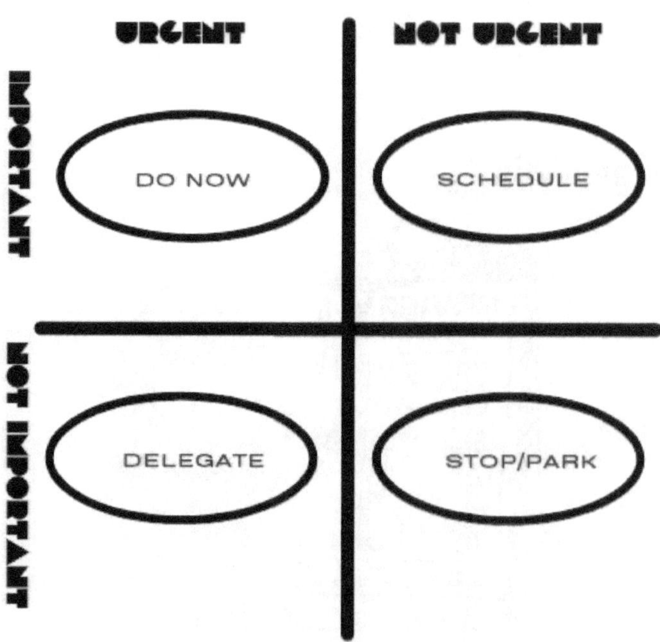

The Eisenhower Matrix helps prioritize tasks by urgency and importance. It divides tasks into four quadrants:

1. **Urgent and Important:** Do these tasks immediately.

2. **Important, Not Urgent:** Schedule these tasks for later.

3. **Urgent, Not Important:** Delegate these tasks if possible.

4. **Not Urgent, Not Important:** Eliminate or minimize these tasks.

By categorizing tasks in this way, you focus on what truly matters, avoid distractions, and ensure you're spending your time on activities that align with your long-term goals. It's an effective tool for managing time and boosting productivity.

*"When you let your priorities guide you,
time becomes less of a constraint. Instead of managing time,
you're aligning it with what's truly important to you."*

Why Steve Jobs cut down Apple's product lines from over 350 to just 10 core products?

In the late 1990s, when Steve Jobs returned to Apple, the company was struggling with a cluttered product line up and declining performance. Jobs decided to simplify the product range and prioritize a few high-impact projects. He famously cut down Apple's product lines from over 350 to just 10 core products. By focusing on fewer, more critical projects, Apple could direct its resources and energy more effectively. This strategic prioritization played a significant role in Apple's turnaround, leading to the development of revolutionary products like the iPod, iPhone, and iPad, and transforming the company into a global leader in technology.

Context switching

If you search in google, the first thing that appears is related to computer world where context switching means the process of switching between different tasks, apps, or projects. Context switching occurs when one process gives way to another process so the second one can be executed. We must understand we are humans, not machines. So in human world, context switching refers to the act of shifting your attention from one task to another, often rapidly and frequently. In today's fast-paced world, where multitasking is common, this concept has become a generic thing in our life. For example, this can include switching between work tasks, checking emails, answering phone calls, or even jumping between different devices, having food while watching mobile/TV etc. But do you think, it's an effective way to manage time or manage life? May be, but each time you switch tasks, there is a cognitive cost—your brain needs time to refocus and reorient itself to the new task. This transition time can reduce productivity, increase errors, and create mental fatigue. These days everyone talks about increased stress, depression. But we don't want to hit the root cause for this. We try to adopt different ways medically, naturally and make our brain effective to handle stress and depression. But we don't want to look at the root cause for this whole thing. Imagine, you have 10 different things to do in a day and you have done a brilliant planning to execute them in a timely manner. You keep doing it without any problem. But what about the side effects of "context switching"? As we age, this takes a severe toll on our mind and health; and create frustration when we can't do this in a longer run.

So, the rule of thumb is – If you have 100 tasks at hand, you can never prioritize things. Just like Steve Jobs, you need to simplify your tasks and reduce it to single digit. Prioritizing helps you stay organized, reduce stress, and make progress on meaningful objectives, leading to better productivity and greater overall satisfaction.

"Time doesn't bend to your schedule; it aligns with your priorities. It's not about managing time, but about setting the right priorities."

Chapter 6

Time is Money - Balancing Hours and Dollars

"Waste your money and you're only out of money
but waste your time and you've lost a part of your life."
~Michael Leboeuf

From Biswajeet's couture

In one of my previous companies where I worked for 4 years, once there was a seminar on financial planning. I still remember those few golden words spoken from the stage by the speaker.

Mr. X: How many of you think that another 10-15K per month would sort all your financial problems?

Audience: More than 90% of people raised their hands.

Mr X: Now tell me, in the last 2-3 years, has your salary increased by that amount or more per month?

Audience: Almost 70% of people said a resounding 'Yes'.

Mr X: Now tell me, have all your financial problems solved?

Audience: 100% of people said 'No'.

Mr X: Is it the amount of money you need or are you missing something here?

The audience had no clue.

Then he began his talk on the importance of financial planning.

As an adult, as a responsible family man, we always think of earning money. Unfortunately, we never think of earning time. Because we have never been told or taught that we should earn time as well. All that was told to us is – we should know how to balance time and money. Believe me, that's the most difficult thing in the material world.

When I decided to earn time

I am a software engineer by profession. When I got my first job for a mere twelve thousand rupees per month, my joy knew no bounds. I shifted the city, left my parents, and left my close friends to start my dream life. I worked really hard, switched companies and increased my salary to five figures. Eventually I got married, travelled to multiple countries, and I thought I am settled quite comfortably now in a metropolitan city. In this journey, one thing I somehow managed is not being a workaholic. Then I got twin kids and my expenses went high. My parents were getting older, and the medical expenses went even further. Then I bought a 2BHK flat on EMI. As a result, expenses skyrocketed.

There was a point, when I was only earning money and wanted to earn even more. So I opted to explore some part-time options. And obviously that resulted in even less time with family. Many times, my wife would fight with me for not giving enough time to her and the two younger ones. And like everyone, I would argue - "I am doing everything for you and the kids only."

Turning point of my life

One summer, my parents visited to stay with me for a few months. My father was diagnosed with a major neurological disorder which had no cure at his age. I did what best could have been done medically. But we knew that he had a few months or years left. They came back to our native place as they were comfortable staying there. Except for money on medicines, I could literally do nothing being 900 miles away from him and that was always bothering me.

One fine day, I decided I must move back to my place. I had four-year-old kids, a house on EMI, and had a bright career ahead. There were not many opportunities back at my native. I used to work at a client place which was the world's numero uno revenue making MNC. When I talked to move out citing personal reasons, I had an open offer to join them with just the double salary which was no doubt lucrative. But thank God, I declined and moved back. Some may consider this as a pure emotional decision, but I was happy with my decision.

"No decision is right or wrong, first you take a decision then only it can be proved wrong or right."

Present day

Both my parents have left for their heavenly abode. But the lifetime satisfaction for me was - when they needed me the most, at their death beds, I was right there, with them. I could have easily shifted back to another metro and started a new career with more money. But the whole sequence of events taught me one thing - I might have earned a few dollars less, but I earned enough time for myself and for my family.

"Everything that happens in our life, happens twice. First in mind and then in actuality."

Navigating through the above wisdom nuggets, Sharda adds on, "I have learnt one significant thing from workplace and family sphere that it is important to maintain a pleasant demeanour without feeling the need to engage in gossips to fit in or please. This is how you disengage from loss of focus, eroded trust of peers and relatives, toxicity and above all, the wasted time. Other than upholding personal integrity, you have more time for productive activities and building strong and trusting relationships. Respectful and constructive communication can influence others to follow the same. Then why not think of engaging in 'skilled time' expenditure to make money? After a short while, 'skilled time' is illustrated for your comprehension.

How much money is enough?

Let's say I earn X amount of money by trading 8 hours per day. And my target is to earn 2X. Here are some questions to ponder.

1. Do you think by trading 16 hours per day, I can make 2X money?

2. Do you think when I make 2X money, life will be settled?

3. Do you think when I earn 2X, my goal would be to make 4X?

4. Where is the end of this race?

In life, we always think if I could earn a little extra money, my life would be settled. Next time you have this thought, find someone who is earning the kind of money you want. Ask him, if life is settled or he also needs that extra little money. We may put forward the logic that, we need to beat the inflation anyways. When I started my career, I was earning a 5-digit income. In less than a decade, I was making 20 times of it. Obviously, inflation on basic needs cannot increase in that proportion. But do you think my life is settled?

"Life is only settled at the death bed."

Be a smart money maker, not a dumb time consumer

Many a times we get confused that more money means more time. Not really. Most of the busy people say this - "Time is money". I partially agree with this. Let me clarify why. Have you seen daily waged labours? They work really hard (almost 10-12 hours) to earn their living just for 3-4 meals a day. If time is money, they should be the richest people on earth.

I think you get the point; someone works the same time as us but may earn less or hell a lot more than us.

So, I would say - "Skilled time is money". One may earn 100/- an hour and the other may earn 1lac an hour. So, it's not about time only, it's about the skills one possesses.

Here are some key points to look at, while we try to balance hours with dollars.

1. Understand the Value of Time as well as Money

In today's world, both time and money have become scarce. But the actual issue is not their scarcity, but how we utilize them both. Time, once lost, cannot be regained whereas money - though finite, can be earned, invested, and multiplied. A "dumb time consumer" means spending time in activities which are either unnecessary or doesn't have any meaning in a long-term growth.

For example, social media, mindless entertainment, procrastination, or engaging in unproductive habits are a few to mention. On the other hand, a "smart money maker" is someone who uses their time strategically to maximize financial opportunities. This does not necessarily mean working 24/7 or being consumed by wealth-building endeavours. It's about being intentional with your time.

2. The Power of Mindset

I always say this – If you want to EARN you have to put a "L" sign board to it, i.e. LEARN. For example, someone who spends an hour each day learning about the stock market or real estate can gradually accumulate valuable knowledge that opens doors to wealth-building opportunities. That's the mindset gap between a smart money maker and a dumb time consumer.

3. Key to financial success – time management

If you want more money, then either you put extra hours or you put smart hours. And we know which one can yield better results. For example, what do you do after office or business hours. Do you watch TV or do you learn something new or do you network with people who are smarter & richer than you. That's what I call effective time management.

4. Passive Income

When I came back to my hometown, I always wanted to do something extra. In fact, in today's world where inflation is rising year on year, surviving on one income is nearly impossible. I tried many things as an extra source of income. When I say I tried, I did the work, not like many who talks about it, but never give it a try. Did I succeed at the first go? No, not at all. But finally, I was able to find out a way where I can build a passive source of income. What is that – an income which can come while you sleep. There are many reference materials and opportunities around for passive income source, You need to expand your thoughts and try multiple things to settle down on your interest area.

5. Long Term thinking

Too often, people fall into the trap of immediate gratification, spending time on short-term pleasures rather than working toward long-term goals. Wealth doesn't accumulate overnight; it requires a series of intentional steps, a willingness to invest time today for a better future.

Treat time as an investment rather than a disposable thing

The way we spend money, if we can create a mindset that every day we are spending time, then achieving both financial success and personal fulfilment will be easier. Treating time as an investment rather than a disposable resource is a mindset that can radically improve productivity and personal fulfilment. Time, once spent, cannot be recovered, making it one of our most valuable assets.

When we view time as an investment, we begin to prioritize activities that align with our long-term goals, growth, and well-being. Just as we would carefully consider where to allocate financial resources, we should also think critically about how we spend our time. This means making intentional decisions, such as dedicating time to learning new skills, fostering relationships, or working on projects that bring personal or professional growth.

On the flip side, when we treat time as disposable, we waste it on mindless activities, distractions, or tasks that don't contribute to our overall well-being. This often leads to regret and burnout, as we feel we have not used our time effectively. Investing time in meaningful and productive endeavours, however, leads to a sense of accomplishment and progress. By being more mindful of how we spend our time and making deliberate choices, we ensure that our days are spent in a way that adds value to our lives, enhances our skills, and helps us move closer to our goals.

"Time is the most valuable currency you have;
spend it wisely, and it will yield you more wealth than
money ever could."

Chapter 7

If You can Manage Time, You can Manage Everything Else in Life

"Time is what we want most,
but what we use worst."
~William Penn

Can you really manage time? You are reading this book; time is passing away. Even if you choose not to read this book at this moment, still time will pass away. You do something or do not, time will still pass away. At first glance, it might seem obvious that we cannot control time. It moves forward relentlessly, and no matter how hard we try, we cannot slow it down or speed it up. The ticking of the clock is beyond our influence, despite this, we find ourselves constantly in pursuit of time: seeking more hours in the day, trying to "find time" for important activities, or lamenting how time slips away too quickly. But in this pursuit, we often miss the point. The one thing we *can* manage is not time itself, but our relationship with time - how we choose to allocate it and what we allow it to define in our lives.

"So, the million-dollar question is - Can you really manage time"? Not really, all you can manage is Yourself".

You read a book on time management, got truly inspired & motivated. To apply the first step of time management, you bought a fancy old alarm clock to inspire you to get up early in the morning. The alarm goes up sharp at 5 AM. You get up, either hit the snooze button or stop the alarm and go back to sleep. What happened there? You did everything right to manage the time, but still failed. The problem is the intention, that is what I call self-management before time management.

"Better Time Management is not a skill to acquire,
it's a result of having an Organised Mindset".

Self-Management is More Important than Time Management

Socrates, one of the famous philosophers of ancient Greece famously declared that

"The unexamined life is not worth living."

We think this applies to how we make decisions related to time. The major challenge with most of us today is we never sit down to examine life. Without self-examination, one may live without a sense of purpose, simply going through the motions of daily existence. In that case, no matter how well we manage time, we can never be fulfilled. Not only that, when situation arises, no time management skills would help. When life is smooth, everyday is going as per your plan, you can plan your day, hours well in advance and it falls into place. But when something goes wrong, life takes a turn, time management skills would go for a toss.

Why Self-Management is more Important?

While time management focuses on the external organization of time and tasks, self-management deals with the internal regulation of one's actions, emotions and priorities. Time management, as a concept, is centred around maximizing the efficiency of one's schedule. However, time is a constant; it ticks forward relentlessly, and no matter how effectively we organize our schedules, the hours of the day are finite. As a result, time management alone cannot compensate for lack of personal discipline or focus, nor can it guarantee that we are working on the right tasks or maintaining the necessary energy levels to complete them. Self-management, on the other hand, refers to the ability to regulate one's thoughts, emotions, and behaviours to achieve desired outcomes.

What killed the youngest CEO?

With a heavy heart, we write this sad real story of one of the youngest CEO in the Indian sub-continent who died after a massive heart attack in his early 40s. That raised a lot of eyebrows not only amongst the doctors, but also in the corporate world. He was very active in sports, was a fitness freak and a marathon runner. His colleagues would proudly say that – He was the master of time; he controlled his time very well. He was a great leader, a great colleague, a smart and intelligent human and go to person for many. He was the idol of many young employees in the corporate world. He did everything right: eating proper food, exercising, maintaining proper weight, balancing hours with dollars.

Hence the question arises as to why an exceptionally active, athletic person succumbed to a heart attack at 40+ years of age.

What everyone missed out is a small line in the reports that said, *"He used to manage with 4-5 hours of sleep."* And statistics says - Individuals who sleep less than 5 hours a night have a 3-fold increased risk of heart attacks. The bottom line is – while he was managing time extraordinarily well, he forgot to manage life.

> *"Managing life over time is not about doing everything, but about doing what truly matters, with intention and balance."*

Managing self and managing time are both crucial for personal productivity and well-being, but they focus on different aspects of how we navigate our lives.

So how do we manage life or self?

1. Life is unpredictable.

Even the most disciplined guy is open to illness, family emergencies, sudden changes in work etc. That is when self-management is crucial. Instead of rigidly adhering to a pre-set agenda, self-managed individuals can reassess their priorities, adjust their expectations, and remain focused on what truly matters in the moment.

For example, when facing a personal crisis or feeling burnt out, self-management allows a person to recognize the need for rest or emotional support and to adjust their goals accordingly. On the contrary, strict time management may only add pressure and greatly reduce productivity.

2. Managing Stress & rejuvenate

Once a reporter asked Mother Teresa - how much time she and her sisters in the Missionaries of Charity spent in prayer and rest. You could be serving so many more people, he told her, if you spent less time praying and resting and more time at work, serving the poor and the sick.

Mother Teresa replied:

Time with God must come first, along with time to rest and rejuvenate to bring the spirit, the energy needed to serve. She said, "With God, I can remember why I do what I do. Then, and only then, am I able to continue my journey, to meet others' needs with a joyful heart."

Taking time to rejuvenate is important for staying healthy and effective. When we work non-stop and face constant stress, we can get burned out, lose creativity, and become less productive. Rejuvenating means giving ourselves a break to relax and recharge. This helps us restore our energy, improve our mood, and handle challenges better. Doing things we enjoy, like hobbies or taking short breaks, can make us feel happier and reduce stress. It also helps keep us from getting sick from too much stress. By making time for rest and relaxation, we not only feel better but also work more efficiently and live a more balanced life. Rejuvenation isn't a luxury—it's a key part of maintaining a healthy, productive, and enjoyable life.

3. Motivation

Almost all of us would have done this at least once in life. Snooze the alarm button and go back to sleep. We want to get up early and continue our daily chores so that we can be effective in time management throughout the day. But still we fail. The only thing that can wake you up in the morning is not the alarm, but the motivation to get up. Without the internal drive to stay committed to the tasks, even the most organized schedules can fall apart.

4. Decision Making

Time management is primarily concerned with the 'how' of getting tasks done, while self-management addresses the 'why.' Effective decision-making requires a clear understanding of one's values, priorities, and long-term vision. That's why a self-managed person can always do time management effectively, but the vice versa may not be always true.

No doubt time management is important, but ultimately, it takes a back seat compared to self-management. Time management provides the structure, but it is self-management that provides the substance - the internal drive, resilience, and emotional intelligence needed.

Either we manage or we don't care

If you are reading this book, you definitely care to change and take control over your time. No one has more than 24 hours a day. And only you can take responsibility of those 24 hours.

Though planning is important, the priority should be execution or the intent behind execution.

Generally, we plan, we fail, and we quit. That's the generic norm. We must rise beyond this plan-fail-quit syndrome. This syndrome, where initial enthusiasm leads to detailed planning, followed by inevitable failure, and culminating in abandonment, can hinder progress and undermine long-term success. To rise beyond this pattern, one must cultivate resilience and adaptability. Instead of seeing failure as an endpoint, view it as a valuable learning experience and an opportunity for recalibration.

Embrace a mindset that values persistence and flexibility over perfection. Recognize that setbacks are not failures but stepping stones towards improvement and eventual success. By setting realistic goals, maintaining a positive outlook, and being open to adjusting strategies as needed, you transform challenges into growth opportunities. Establishing a supportive network and seeking constructive feedback can also provide the necessary encouragement and perspective to keep moving forward. Ultimately, rising beyond the "plan-fail-quit" syndrome, involves developing a resilient attitude, staying committed to your objectives, and continuously evolving through every trial and error.

How Steve Jobs managed life to manage his time

Steve Jobs, renowned for his innovation and productivity, had several key strategies for managing time effectively:

Focus on Priorities: Jobs was known for his ability to prioritize what mattered most. He believed in concentrating on a few critical projects rather than spreading himself too thin. This approach allowed him to devote significant energy and resources to tasks that could have the greatest impact.

Say No: Jobs famously said that the ability to say no is crucial to maintaining focus. By rejecting less important projects or ideas, he could ensure that his attention remained on the most valuable opportunities.

Embrace Simplicity: Jobs valued simplicity in both product design and workflow. He believed that by stripping away the non-essential, he could focus on creating meaningful and innovative solutions. This principle extended to how he managed his time, emphasizing the importance of clarity and purpose.

Deep Work: Jobs often immersed himself deeply in his work, focusing intensely on the task at hand. This practice of deep work allowed him to make significant progress on complex problems and achieve high levels of productivity.

Passion and Vision: Jobs' passion for his work and his clear vision for Apple's future drove him to manage his time with purpose. His dedication to his goals ensured that he used his time efficiently to advance his company's mission.

The only thing you can manage in life is time

It may sound contradictory but think about it. Can you manage life situations? Can you manage death? Can you manage your kids? Can you manage people around you? To some extent yes, when you have authority as a parent, as a boss or as a leader. But practically it's not in our control. That's why we say, the only thing that we can manage is "TIME". We cannot control its passage, but we can manage how we spend it. Noone has the control over your time except you. Yes, we are occupied in jobs or business or studies, we have a family to run and other social responsibilities which would consume time in our day-to-day life. But ultimately, it's our time, so the choice should be ours only. While time is a finite resource, it is also the medium through which we experience life itself. The way we choose to spend our time determines the direction of our lives and the meaning we find in them.

The key to understanding why time is the only thing we can truly manage in life lies in recognizing that it is finite. Unlike money or material possessions, time is the one resource that cannot be accumulated or replenished. Once a moment has passed, it is gone forever. We cannot "store" time for later use, and we cannot undo the choices we made in past moments. Every person on this planet is given the same 24 hours in a day, yet the way we use that time can vastly differ from one person to the next.

Are you running out of time?

Are we truly running out of time, or are we simply mismanaging it? While it's easy to feel like we're running out of time, a shift in perspective can help. At its core, the feeling of running out of time often arises from poor time management or the inability to prioritize tasks effectively. Many people today juggle multiple responsibilities — work, family, personal development, and more — which can create a sense of being overwhelmed.

The constant barrage of tasks and demands, combined with distractions, can lead to the perception that there is never enough time to accomplish everything. However, when we break down our day into specific tasks and set clear priorities, we begin to realize that we have more control over our time than we think.

The finite nature of time often leads to feelings of anxiety or pressure. We may feel as though we are running out of time to accomplish our goals or live the life we desire. But this sense of urgency is not necessarily a bad thing. It can serve as a reminder of the preciousness of every passing moment and the importance of using our time wisely. By acknowledging that time is limited, we can begin to make more deliberate choices about how we use it.

"Mastering time is the key to mastering life;
when you control your moments, you unlock the
potential to shape your destiny."

Who has Time?

I am a software Engineer, I Don't have Time

How a software engineer's day looks like, in a metro, these days.

Travel to office => Tea break => Morning stand-up => Lunch break => After lunch walk => Chit chat => Tea break => Meeting => Travel back to home => Meetings

Surely you are smiling if you are a software engineer and reading this.

For software engineers, the concept of work life balance doesn't work. The nature of work demands flexible timings. The more flexible you are, the better the appraisal. The more weekends you work, the happier the client would be. So, for software engineers, they coined a new term – "Work Life Integrity".

What is work life Integrity?

Couple of years back, Biswajeet attended a seminar on Work-Life Balance. There the speaker talked about this new concept.

Work-life integrity refers to the alignment and harmony between a person's professional responsibilities and personal life, with an emphasis on maintaining a balance that reflects personal values, well-being, and authenticity. Unlike work-life balance, which often suggests a strict division between work and personal life, work-life integrity focuses on integration and ensuring that both areas support and complement each other, rather than causing conflict.

Key aspects of work-life integrity include:

1. Authenticity: Ensuring that your work and personal life reflect your true values and principles, without compromising on either side.

2. Consistency: Maintaining a sense of integrity in both your professional and personal roles. For example, if you prioritize honesty in your personal life, you will aim to do the same at work.

3. Boundaries and Flexibility: Setting boundaries that protect your personal time while also being flexible enough to meet work demands, when necessary, without feeling that one area of your life is being neglected.

4. Fulfilment and Well-being: Striving for a sense of satisfaction and fulfilment in both work and life, recognizing that both contribute to your overall happiness and sense of purpose.

In essence, work-life integrity is about living in a way that reflects a balance of priorities, where neither work nor personal life dominates, and both are managed in ways that allow you to thrive. It's a more holistic, values-driven approach to manage the complexities of modern life.

Here are some approaches that can be adopted and are crucial if you are a software engineer.

1. Learn to Say NO

This is very important if you are a software engineer. Of course, this is an important aspect of time management for everyone, but for engineers, it's the most important. In the quest of good appraisal, generally you tend to accept anything and everything that comes your way. But you have to realise your limits and accordingly accept the tasks on hand. Being at higher position, Biswajeet can relate to it as many a times we tend to give extra work to test the stretching limits of a resource. The more you stretch, more we tend to give. It's tempting to take on additional tasks or attend all meetings, but not every opportunity is valuable or urgent. Learn to say no to tasks that don't align with your priorities or goals.

2. Delegate and Collaborate

This is another important aspect of an engineer's life. When I was riding on the corporate ladder, Biswajeet was told by his superiors at work – if you want to go up, you must learn how to delegate. Individual contributors are many, but only those go up who knows how to effectively get the work done and this is really vital for your time management. So, if you love to do just your work on your own, take a break and start delegating. And don't reinvent the wheel. We are at an era, where nothing is newly implemented. If you can collaborate well at least within your organization across different teams, you can find a much better solution at a very lesser time.

3. Limit Interruptions & distractions

As we started this topic with the regular software engineer's day to day life, this is very prevalent. Taking breaks is definitely important but knowing the limits and knowing how many breaks are actually required will determine how long you need to work every day.

4. Leverage Tools and Automation

This is bread and butter for software engineers, but the problem is they only know to automate things when they are asked in their work. Outside work, it is just the regular human working day and night. There are plenty of tools available in your organization itself which can reduce your daily work to certain extent. For example, many developers struggle with excel sheet or reporting. Learn it to reduce the time spent on these tasks. Automate repetitive tasks which will free up time for more critical tasks and improves overall efficiency.

5. Minimize Context Switching

The higher you go; the more responsibility is thrown on your shoulders. Many struggle to cope up with these roles and some do it smoothly. The difference is how effective you are in context switching. Focus on time blocking for different projects and group similar tasks.

6. Set SMART Goals

They call it SMART as it decodes to Specific, Measurable, Achievable, Relevant, Time-bound. Theoretically you might know this as part of some training or during the beginning of the year when your manager sets goals for you. But have you ever set your own goals; doesn't happen that with many. As they think, it's not their responsibility, it's manager's headache to take care of them. Frankly, this determines how well you plan the year if you set your own goals, rather than working towards what has been set by someone else for you.

7. Take Advantage of Downtime

We don't say go out on vacation or trek with friends or party hard. Because that's default with software engineers. As most of the companies have weekend off, so they are good at planning all of the above whenever they get a chance. The productive usage of downtime would be to review documentation, learn new technologies, or brainstorm solutions. This may sound like a manager's advice, but believe me, on a longer run, this is what matters which the deadlines bounce on your head.

8. Maintain a Clean and Organized Workspace

Again, this is an attitudinal aspect. If your desk is messy, that reflects on your personality. People think you are too busy, and that creates the negative energy around you. Everyday 5 minutes, that's all it takes to have a clean and clutter-free desk.

I am a Doctor, I am Not Supposed to Have Time

The famous Doctor & the mechanic story

One afternoon, in a busy garage filled with the scent of oil and the hum of engines, a mechanic was hard at work, carefully removing a cylinder head from a motorcycle's motor. His hands were deep in the task, focused on the intricate work of disassembling the engine. As he worked, he happened to glance across the garage and saw a familiar face — Dr. Johnson, a well-known cardiologist, was waiting for the service manager to inspect his bike. The mechanic paused for a moment, a thought forming in his mind.

"Hey Doc, want to take a look at this?" the mechanic called out across the room.

The cardiologist, surprised by the invitation, walked over from where he was standing, curious about what the mechanic wanted to show him. He made his way to the workbench, where the mechanic had set aside the engine components. The mechanic wiped his hands on a rag, stood up straight, and gestured toward the disassembled engine.

"Take a look at this," the mechanic began. "I open up the engine's heart, take out the valves, repair any damage I find, and then put everything back together. Once I'm done, the engine runs like new. Now, tell me this—why is it that I make $30,000 a year, and you, doing what seems like the same kind of work, pull in over half a million a year?"

The cardiologist stood still for a moment, thinking over the mechanic's question. After a short pause, he smiled and leaned in closer, as if sharing a secret. "Well," the cardiologist said, his voice soft but confident, "try doing it with the engine running."

We always have a deep respect towards doctors as they are the first type of human beings who can save lives. The other type who can make lives – well, we will talk about them in the next section.

With due respect, we still feel that – doctors are really great in managing lives, but not that great in managing time. Yes, it's true that when you are managing life, that takes priority over time. But that doesn't give the doctors the liberty to not manage their time itself. Here is a situation which almost everyone would have faced at least once in their lives.

Doctor's appointment

If the doctor is reputed, then you know the difficulty to get an appointment. However, after multiple attempts, you finally got the doctor's appointment for your kid in one of the Multi-speciality hospitals in your town. They ask you to reach before 15 mins. Being disciplined, you reach before 30 minutes. You opened the door, and you see the room is filled with people — some were flipping through magazines, others were glued to their phones, and a few quietly chatted with one another.

You immediately realised it's going to be another long wait. You approach the reception desk to check in and the receptionist calmly says – I am sorry, the doctor is running a bit late. You try to find a chair and be comfortable glancing around the waiting area. You read all the healthy tips written in the colourful wall. You check your social media messages while your kid starts playing games in his Tab. Suddenly you look at the wristwatch to find out that it's already one hour.

You lose a little bit of your patience and walk to the receptionist to ask: "how much more time it would take". Once again, the receptionist in a very calm voice replies: "The doctor will be here any time, please wait, we will call you."

Finally, after some more waiting, you hear your kid's name being called out. You walk down the corridor with your kid and enter the examination room, you can't help but think about the absurdity of it all. You waited nearly an hour waiting for just a 5-minute check-up. But as soon as you enter the room and greet the doctor, all the frustration melts away. Despite the wait, you know that the doctor's expertise and attention to detail made the time spent waiting worthwhile. And you leave the hospital happily after the check-up.

Can this be better?

I know this experience is very normal for the patient, but do you think this can be better? We totally agree, there can be emergency situations which the doctor must attend first, but many a times it is not. Of course, the emergency situations cannot be dealt with any options, but we feel the system can be much better to provide a better experience and better time management. Unless it's an immediate emergency, the patient can be informed about the doctor's unexpected delay. How can you do that with so many patients waiting for you? We recommend – If software can be used to take appointments, the same software can be used to send a broadcast message and even better, can reschedule the appointment to reduce the waiting time of the patient. A simple solution, but not thought of yet.

"When a doctor is late, he is not late alone, along with him, all his patients and their attendants get late as well."

Can a Doctor Manage His Time?

Barring emergency situations, every doctor still struggles to manage time and it's not always due to the heavy demand. At the end of the day, a doctor also has a family, and he is a normal human being with full of emotions. Here are some tips which can be used.

1. Prioritize Tasks and Appointments

2. Create a Structured Schedule

3. Delegate Administrative Tasks

4. Limit Distractions During Patient Consultations

5. Use Technology to Streamline Processes

6. Incorporate Buffer Time

7. Set Realistic Time Limits

8. Avoid Multitasking

9. Take Breaks to Recharge

Definitely, a doctor can apply the above techniques to manage time, but the ultimate truth is, he or she needs to accept the fact that they can manage time. Not only you, but the whole society also thinks that you are busy. And that's not a good sign. Just imagine, what kind of energy you are gathering around you – "I am busy and the whole world thinks that I am right."

Next time when you feel you should break this jinx, here are some points to retrospect.

1. You are not the only doctor in your specialized area.

2. You don't need to attend every function that you are invited to.

3. Unlike other professions, you have the whole life to earn money, so slow down.

4. Ask yourself – How much is enough?

5. Stop comparing yourself with other doctors. We say this, as this is most common with doctors.

6. Stop being jealous of other doctors with your speciality.

7. You don't need to impress anyone other than your family and your patients.

I am a Businessman; It Only means A Man with Busyness.

Biswajeet unfolds

Couple of years back, I was very keen on starting my own business. I think all engineers have this dream of their own.

After becoming an engineer, they want to do everything except engineering work. So, when I was evaluating what businesses can make me great profit in less time (at least a job holder thinks this way), people around me advised to try a medicine shop. I was excited as I knew the margins on medicines are really huge. But then reality hit me on my face. When I deep dived about running a medicine store, what I realised is – you have to sit at the counter from the time it opens till the time you put the shutters down. Then I realised, why businessmen are so busy in their field. No doubt, they own the business, but the fear of employee/staff always bothers them in the back of their mind.

How many times you might have heard this from a businessman or shopkeeper – the moment I leave the counter or as soon as I take a vacation, when I am back everything would be upside down. That's why I hate taking leaves/long leaves.

Practically being a businessman is not easy, and when you are at the beginning of your business career, that's the most crucial phase. That's why time management is really critical for a businessman, as it directly impacts productivity, decision-making, and overall success. Very few can do this and very few learn to do this in a longer period of time. But one thing which is common is – they are super busy. Comparing job with business is like comparing apple with oranges. Jobs demand fixed time with fixed delivery. No matter what, salary is credited at the end of the month. No accounting, no account payable or receivable. But business demands a lot of things to be managed. So, unless it's a family business, at the beginning, management becomes the biggest issue which leads to a stressful life. After some time, it becomes a habit or daily chore of your life. And people happily accept that business means overtime and stress.

But if you look at successful businessmen, they know how to manage. I know they might not have started like that. But at least we can refer to their stories and build on top of that. People always think that – my business is not that big, so I have to manage a lot of things on my own. Wrong, because you are managing a lot of things on your own, your business doesn't stand a chance to grow or scale up.

My financial mentor always tells me this.

Mentor: Do you see that medicine store at the corner?

Me: Yes, it's been there from a long time.

Mentor: It was there when I was a child and it's still there when my kid is going to school.

Me: Wow, great.

Mentor: Not really.

Me: Oh, but why? They are doing really well financially.

Mentor: Don't you see the scalability issue?

Me: You mean from generations they are managing one single store though the size has increased.

Mentor: Absolutely. If your presence decides the fate of your business, then you don't own it, the business owns you. Practically you are not a businessman, you are just self-employed.

And when you are self-employed, you won majority of the work being done. Without your presence the whole business system may collapse. And that's whole reason of businessmen being busy or stressed. The question is can you deal with it? Absolutely yes.

Here are some practical strategies a businessman can use to manage time more effectively:

1. Set Clear Priorities

Identify Key Objectives: Understand what truly drives the success of your business. Focus on tasks that align with these objectives. Focus on what matters most and delegate or eliminate the rest. The problem with most small-scale businessmen is that they fear to delegate. One you learn of art of delegation; you would have ample time to enjoy both the business and personal life.

2. Plan and Schedule

Though this is applicable for all professions, but for businessmen it's a priority task as they are not liable to anyone to adhere to a plan or schedule. Time blocking, daily and weekly Planning, breaking down larger tasks into smaller one, using digital tools - all can help manage time effectively.

3. Automation

This is a common phenomenon with small scale business owners, they fail to adapt and use technology to their advantage.

Use software tools to automate routine business functions such as invoicing, email responses, inventory management, or payroll processing. At a minimum, use WhatsApp effectively to manage resources and save time.

4. Learn to Say No

Everyone would agree with this, no businessman like to say No and in the process they overcommit.

Overcommitting is the bread and butter for every businessman. Saying "no" is a key part of protecting your time, energy and stress level. There is no issue in looking up the sky but be realistic to have your feet grounded.

5. Take Breaks and Rest

Schedule regular breaks throughout the day. Incorporate exercise, proper nutrition, and sleep into your routine to keep your mind and body in optimal condition.

There can many more tips to incorporate, but if one can adhere to the above five points, then majority of the time issues would be managed, and you can definitely lead a stress-free life.

I am a Teacher; My Students Take Away All My Time.

"Teaching is a vocation, not 'just' a job."

Whoever coined the phrase "find a job you love, and you'll never work a day in your life" was right, at least for the teaching profession. A teacher without the love for his or her work most likely struggles to balance out work and life.

In a typical day a teacher might prepare materials, assess student work and provide feedback, contact parents, plan lessons, make photocopies, attend meetings, provide extra support to students, troubleshoot technology issues, prepare displays of student work, maintain an interesting and tidy classroom, enter grades into a school management system, write student reports, supervise a detention, attend to a scraped knee/ nose bleed, and complete multitudes of 'essential' paperwork. Oh, and amongst all of that, teach a full day of back-to-back classes, perhaps with an after-school parents evening for good measure.

If reading that list made you breathless, it was meant to. That's how teachers feel all day, every day. And you can't do all these without the love for the profession unless money is a dire need. Sharda has been a teacher for more than 15 years now. She believes what Chanakya had once said, "Teachers build nations." If we delve deep, we need to acknowledge that we are actually thrusted with the biggest responsibility to educate future leaders through transfer of knowledge, encouraging critical thinking and nurturing leadership qualities in them. The list does not end here. Fostering civic responsibilities, teaching to resolve conflicts, inspiring innovation, imparting values of honesty, integrity, respect and responsibility and many more. Therefore, somebody has rightly said "A teacher affects eternity; he can never tell where his influence stops". In achieving all this one needs to be consumed in the process of lighting ways for others.

Biswajeet's mother was a high school teacher. While growing up, he too has seen how busy she used to be managing school, home and his dad's sudden plans. But he never saw her complain a bit for time. Yes, she used to say that she had always her plate full of work, but she never complained she had no time.

What we can learn from Biswajeet's mother & Dr. Sharda

1. She never complained about time

We were three kids at home. My father was a PSU employee, and my mother was a high school teacher. Her shift would be from 11AM – 5PM. When I was in primary school in the morning school, my sister was in high school. I remember, I used to go to school by 7 AM. So, my mother's day would start at 5 AM in the morning and ended somewhere around 11 PM at night. She would be as energetic as she was in the morning even while going to bed. I always used to think, where from she got so much energy. Today when I look back, I feel it was her "Never Complain" attitude which kept her always going. You ask her for a evening ritual, ask for a weekend meet, so would be always ready.

2. She was a master in delegating work

Most teachers do that at school, but they lack the ability to share load at home. I used to get annoyed when my dad sweeps home or wash the utensils when our maid was off, but now I realise that was a proper way of running a happy family by sharing the load. And my mother was really great at doing that gracefully, not forcefully. As a 7-year-old kid, when I get back from school, I used to serve my own meal, have it and put back the utensils in the sink. I don't remember how I did that when I look at my kids. That culture must have been set by my mother – be self-independent at home. And believe me, these small tasks free you up to manage bigger responsibilities. We always had a maid at home while growing up, I remember I started my tuitions at standard one itself. But those were required for my mother so that she can manage many more kids at school without any stress.

As a professor and a supervisor for PhD students, Sharda recollects her own PhD days at NIT, Rourkela. How she was given autonomy to explore and bring fresh perspectives by her madam supervisor thus creating a collaborative and empowering research environment. She was delegated tasks to develop essential research skills, including data collection, analysis and critical thinking. Mistakes and roadblocks always stared at her. However, she gradually learnt to manage time, resources and tasks efficiently. She had to, as she was about to deliver her baby during her thesis writing days. Thesis needed completion before becoming a 24-hr caregiving mother. So now she has learnt that distributing work among scholars ensures that the projects progress smoothly and the deadlines are met. When they take ownership of their work, they are more engaged and committed to the project's success.

3. She had her own ways to manage stress

These days if you look at different professions, teachers compete at the top level to manage stress. My mother knew to handle it very nicely. She was spiritually well connected, of course that gave her that inner strength which goes missing for many teachers these days. On top of that, she knew to smile. Believe me, today when I meet my friends who also studied in the same school, they could only memorise my mother's smiling face. Smile, it costs nothing, but it can heal a lot of things in life was the mantra for her.

4. She was organized and made us likewise

My wife always tells me this – how can you be so organized. I smile and look back my childhood days. In our home, even if a small needle is missing, my mother would exactly know where it is. Even in sleep if you ask her where one particular thing is which has not been used for months or years, she would exactly pin point where she kept it. You may think how does it help in time management. Big time, if you are a mother of two kids, you can relate to it. Just imagine how much time you spend finding the notebooks or small items. Not only that, at crunch times, it becomes stressful as well. When you are organized, kids grow up that way and a lot of time can be saved.

5. She was selfish

No, don't take it otherwise. She used to have her personal space where she never allowed anyone to interfere. She used to find time for herself to rejuvenate. As a teacher, when you are occupied whole day with kids, students – you don't want to come back home and look at another one. She was good at using those hidden hours of the day when I would be out playing, or my sister would be out for tuitions. She used to have her favourite snacks all alone. It may sound silly, but believe me, that gives you a lot of satisfaction. I am not saying you should not share or care, but as a person you always should have your personal space and for teachers this means a lot.

Sharda adds that in case of a professor, by saying a 'no', we model assertive behaviour and boundary setting for our students, which are important life skills. In addition to this, setting clear boundaries with a 'no' helps maintain respect and authority in the classroom. It shows students and colleagues that you have limits, and your time and energy are valuable. At the semester ending, B. Tech students are awarded sessional and internal marks which are solely in our hands. Some carefree ones do not bother to complete the assignments and ask for grace marks to get cumulative good grades. Sharda tells them granting unearned grace marks can set a precedent, leading other students to expect the same treatment which shall erode the academic standards of the institution. In addition, it will be unfair to other students who have completed their assignments and adhered to the rules. So, a strict 'no' is the only response.

6. She made the most of classroom time

I must say she was a master in that. I have seen many teachers struggle in checking the students copies or exam papers. She used to finish that in the school itself. Either during leisure period or during the adjustment periods, she would finish this. I never saw her bringing students copies back home. Now that's what I call effective time management.

7. She was a great collaborator

I have seen many teachers struggle to adjust their classes during emergencies. My mother used to be very good at putting up her request to her colleagues and get her work done. None the less, she used to help other teachers selflessly at their time of need. She was loving and she was loved by not only the students, but by the teachers as well.

I always had and will have a soft corner for the teacher fraternity not only because my mother was teacher, but because

I always feel a great teacher can build a great nation. They are creator of the foundation of our society. So, I feel they should be stress free and in a positive mindset always and time management can help teachers big time.

I am a Student, I Need More Time

Time management for a student is the process of planning and organizing how to allocate time effectively for different academic, personal, and extracurricular tasks. It is crucial for achieving academic success, reducing stress, and maintaining a balanced lifestyle. Most of the time, a student is scared only because of exams and that is when he or she realises the importance of time management. But if you approach the whole year as a package and accordingly plan for it, you would never be in a situation where time is a shortage for you. Of course, other techniques apply to a student for time management, but the most important thing is to plan the whole year.

Take one year as a package

When an academic year begins, it is a fresh new year for you. If you can utilise the whole year effectively, there could be no exam fear in mind. But how do we achieve that? Here are some tips for you to take the whole year package.

1. Forget last year even if you have topped the exam or just passed it or even failed.

2. In the whole year package, one thing is must – attending classes regularly. You must be thinking what is new about it. New thing is – do not just listen, always attend a class with notebook and a pen.

3. Every day before you go to sleep – just go through the chapter that was taught in the class. You do not need to focus on remembering the whole chapter, just go through it.

4. Have a copy of your own which would be the replica of the book. Whenever you are bored or you need to study just for the sake of sitting down, take this copy and start writing the chapter. Yes, the whole chapter.

5. Imagine you are the examiner, and you need to set the questions for next year for your student. As you are a good

teacher, you want to give your student all the questions that are possible from one chapter. Write down all the possible questions from a chapter. Just the questions.

6.   Fix a time every day, just one hour and name it as "Exam Prep Time". Take one chapter and do an exam like preparation. Believe it or not, if you can do this 5 days a week, you do not need to be scared for the exam.

7.   Another tip which is recommended – Have a notebook, name it "Five pages copy". Write 5 pages every day from 5 different topics. It can be some Q/A, some notes, or some piece for the book. Make sure you cover five different topics every day.

One month before the exam

The most critical time for any student: Exam. This is where the difference in grades appear. If you have followed the tips for the whole year, then this one month should be no different. But if you have not taken the annual package, then you must take the monthly package.

1.   Prepare a calendar for one month. Every day cross one day from it and it should be visible to you all the time.

2.   Count all the chapters from all the books. Divide that by 30 and program your brain for this daily cycle for next one month.

3.   Prepare a one-month diary where you can put the daily schedule at a higher level. Remember, you are your best guide.

4.   You must be eyeing at late night studies and long hour studies. But frankly that helps less. You can read the "I

am a night owl" chapter from the book "What If Exams Were Not There" to get more insights on this.

5. Manage your breaks. Here is what we suggest during long hours. Every 15 minutes take a 2-minute break. After each one hour take a 10-minute break. This can yield more output.

6. Your play time should not be compromised. One hour every day is must. Never spend that hour on mobile games. Make sure you go out, meet your friends, or play outside.

7. When you start reading a chapter:

   1. Gather the notes that you have prepared.

   2. Get the Q/A copy that you wrote during the year.

   3. Get the last 10-year Q/A copy.

   4. Here is the sequence to completely revise a chapter.

      i. Read the whole chapter (If you have not done so far)

      ii. Read the notes and then glance through the chapter.

      iii. Go through the Q/A copy of your own.

      iv. Go through the 10-year Q/A copy.

8. Whenever you sit down o study, think of the chapter as your last nail in the coffin. Imagine you have only this chapter for the exam and go for the best preparation.

> *"Drop by drop fills the ocean and*
> *every drop counts."*

You see, if you have completed the annual package, this one month will just be a cakewalk for you. Otherwise, this one month can become a nightmare. A lot depends on how you have utilised the whole year. Every small effort throughout the year counts. Most of the time we think -

- Today I am very tired, from tomorrow I will start reading.

- After this vacation, I will start with full force.

- After my sister's marriage I will be serious.

- This year I could not study. Next year I will start afresh.

- Once this league matches are over, I will study day and night.

Does that happen? Even if you read few lines from the book on a tiring day that has effect on a long run. Here is a well known story from the Ramayan which can refresh your mind and make you realise the effect of small efforts.

Rama asked his army to build the bridge over the sea. The monkeys pulled out rocks and heavy stones from the mountains and carried them to the sea. They cut them into shape and began to build the bridge. This was a very difficult task to undertake. Hundreds of monkeys worked day and night. One day, Rama saw a small brown squirrel. He was going up and down the seashore with little pebbles in his mouth and sand on his back. The little squirrel could carry only small pebbles at a time in his small mouth. He carried the pebbles from the seashore and dropped them into the sea.

A giant monkey was carrying a heavy stone on his back and the squirrel came in his way. The monkey jumped back: Hey you little thing, shouted the monkey what are you doing here?

The little squirrel looked up at the great monkey.

Bro, I am really sorry to come in your way, he said in his small voice, but I am helping Rama build the bridge.

"You, what?" shouted the monkey and laughed aloud. "Did you hear that!" he said to the other monkeys. "The little squirrel is helping us to build the bridge with his pebbles. Oh dear! Oh dear! I've never heard a funnier story." The other monkeys laughed too.

The monkeys said, "Don't be foolish. Do you think you can help Rama? Do you think we can build a bridge with pebbles? He has a big army to help him. Go home and don't get in our way."

"But I want to help, too," said the squirrel and continued its work.

One of the monkeys got angry and picked up the squirrel by his tail and threw him far away.

The squirrel, crying out the name of Rama, fell into his hands.

Then Rama held the squirrel close to him.

He said to the monkeys, "Do not make fun of the weak and the small. You are brave and strong and are doing a wonderful job bringing all these huge boulders and stones from far and dropping them in the ocean. But did you notice that it is the tiny pebbles and stones brought by this small squirrel which are filling the small gaps left between the huge stones? Further, do you realize that the tiny grains of sand brought by this squirrel are the ones which bind the whole structure and make it strong?"

Do you see the importance of small efforts? When you use those 10 minutes for your study, even that adds value at the end of the year. So, it's not the bigger chunks of time that make the difference, at the end, it's always the small ones that differentiate you from others.

I am a Banker, The Toughest Job I have, Don't Ask Me for Time

While growing up, we had two major career options – a doctor and an engineer. Along with those, there was one more job which caught everyone's attention as a 9-5 job – a banker. If you are a banker and reading this, you want to give us a piece of your mind. We totally understand that. With the advent of technology, modernisation and privatization the competition to stay on the job has become very tight, not only for the staff, but also for the bank itself. In today's world, the world of banking is filled with tight deadlines, intricate processes, and high stakes. It is a career that requires not only skill and expertise but also an unyielding sense of discipline and time management.

A banker always says this –

"Despite the importance of time in my profession, one of the most frustrating aspects of my job is when people, including clients, family, and friends, ask me for more of it. The reality is that, as a banker, time is a luxury I often cannot afford."

We totally agree with him or her as banking is a demanding profession in many ways, primarily defined by the enormous responsibility of managing people's money, handling financial risk, and ensuring the smooth operation of transactions that can range from routine savings deposits to multimillion-dollar loans. The nature of the job itself demands that bankers work long hours, sometimes stretching well beyond the traditional nine-to-five.

How can I manage time

Time management is essential in every profession, but for bankers, it is absolutely crucial. The demanding nature of banking requires professionals to do multiple tasks, meet deadlines, and respond to clients quickly. As a result, managing time effectively not only ensures that a banker remains productive but also helps maintain a work-life balance and reduces the stress associated with the work. Almost all the strategies are required as far as a banker is concerned to effectively manage time. But more than that, the stress management is important for banking professionals as they deal with two most important aspects of this world – "MONEY" and "HUMANS". All the following time management techniques can be used, but something is more important than these.

- Prioritize Tasks
- Time Blocking
- Setting Realistic Goals and Deadlines
- Delegate and Collaborate
- Learn to Say No
- Use Downtime Wisely
- Reflect and Adjust

More than any other professions, bankers need to do this first.

REMOVE THE MENTAL BLOCK THAT I AM BUSY

1. Shift Your Focus from Busyness to what you're actually accomplishing
2. Stop Procrastination
3. Practice Mindfulness and Self-Reflection
4. Reframe Your Thoughts on Time
5. Accept That You Can't Do Everything
6. Practice meditation

I am a Housewife, Mother of Kid(s), I am the Busiest Person in the World

Recently a video on social media went viral. The boy's family visits the girls house for the first time and here is the conversation between the mother of the boy and the girl who is supposed to marry and shift house.

MIL – Do you know how to cook?

Girl – Oh yes, I can cook Indian, continental and I am taking online Chinese cooking classes.

MIL – Wow, wonderful, how about cleaning clothes.

Girl – I know how to operate automatic and semi-automatic washing machines, also I am comfortable with manual machines. And soft clothes, I prefer to do it with my own hands.

MIL – I see the house is very neatly organised. Is it you who have maintained the house so beautifully?

Girl – Of course yes, vacuuming, dusting, and sweeping the floors are my core strengths. And I don't like to see any corners in the house dirty.

MIL (overwhelmingly asked) – I think she is just perfect for our son. We are ok to accept this proposal.

Suddenly the daughter gets up and asked,

Girl – But you didn't tell me how much salary I would get?

Everyone in the room was silently stunned.

Most of the housewives create this mental block on themselves. Not only the society feels that housewives have no job, but the lady in the house herself is convinced that she is not earning, so she must do all the possible or impossible household work. Believe me, in today's world, if you are managing two kids at home, that's no less than doing a full-time job with no appreciation. Job holders just do some work, but you are building a life at home. I wish housewives get some recognition in the real world for all their hard work. Having said that, here are few tips for all you beautiful housewives to manage your time, manage your life and enjoy being a home maker.

1. Delegate When Possible

Delegating doesn't mean you're failing; it's a smart way to manage your responsibilities, ensuring that you have time for both your duties and self-care. Involve family members, hire help when needed, outsource tasks, use technology and set realistic expectations.

2. Take Time for Yourself

Just like any other role, your health and mental well-being matter. Set aside time daily or weekly for activities that refresh you, whether it's reading, taking a walk, meditating, or enjoying a hobby. By taking time for yourself, you'll not only feel more rejuvenated but also be able to give your best to others in your home. Self-care is a key part of being able to care for your family and household.

3. Limit the Social Distractions

Allocate specific times during the day or week for social interactions, whether it's phone calls, social media, or meeting friends. Avoid letting these activities interfere with household tasks or personal time. By managing your social distractions, you can be more productive, maintain a healthy balance, and have quality time for both your responsibilities and social connections.

4. Learn to Say No

You don't have to be rude when saying no. You can politely explain that you're unable to take on a task or commitment at the moment. For example, "I'd love to help, but I'm already committed to something else right now." By learning to say "no," you maintain control over your schedule, reduce stress, and ensure that you're giving your best to the things that truly matter. It's a powerful way to protect your time and energy.

5. Plan Your Meals

As a housewife, I think this is the most time-consuming task. If you can manage this, I am pretty sure, you would get a superb control over your time. Create a weekly menu, make a shopping list, prepare and cook in bulk as & when possible, involve the family, use leftovers creatively and stay flexible. By planning your meals ahead of time, you'll save time, reduce stress, and be able to create nutritious, cost-effective meals for your family while enjoying the process.

6. Make Use of Free Time

Making use of your free time effectively not only enhances personal well-being but also allows you to feel more balanced, productive, and fulfilled. Most of the time I see, housewives take small breaks but use them in social media which at times creates even more stress. Here are some ideas for how to make the most of your free time – learn new skills, exercise and stay active, relax and recharge, organize and de-clutter, socialize and build relationships (of course not for gossips), focus on personal stuff, relax and pamper yourself, focus on your passion.

7. Don't Be Too Hard on Yourself

As a housewife, it's easy to fall into the trap of being overly critical of yourself. There's often pressure to manage everything perfectly –

household chores, cooking, child-rearing, and other responsibilities. However, it's important to remember that you don't have to do it all perfectly, and being kind to yourself is crucial for your well-being. Here are some ways to avoid being too hard on yourself. Remember, being a housewife is a demanding role, and you are doing important work. Don't be too hard on yourself; focus on doing your best and taking care of your own needs too.

8. Get Healthy, Get Active

I am sure you must have heard or told this – I am working so much every day, still I am unable to manage my weight. As a housewife, it's easy to get caught up in managing household tasks and caring for others, but it's equally important to prioritize your own health and well-being. Here are some simple and effective ways to get healthy and active – Incorporate exercise into daily routine, eat a balanced diet, make time for relaxation, prioritize sleep, get outdoors, engage in mental health activities.

9. Reward Yourself

Rewarding yourself as a housewife is an important practice for maintaining balance, motivation, and self-care. Amidst daily tasks and responsibilities, it's easy to forget to appreciate the hard work you put into managing the home and caring for your family. Here are some simple ways to reward yourself

– Unwind with a hobby, pamper yourself, acknowledge your efforts, enjoy your favourite snack or dessert, schedule a "me day" (a day off from all household work), socialize with your old friends, buy something you always wanted, enjoy a relaxing movie or TV show if you like, take a nap.

10. Learn to Let Go

As a housewife, it's easy to feel overwhelmed with the constant flow of responsibilities—caring for the family, managing household chores, cooking, and more. One important way to maintain your well-being is learning to **let go** of the pressure to do it all perfectly and to release the need for control over every situation. Let go of control, let go of comparing yourself to others, let go of past mistakes, let go of stress, let go of the idea of being a "supermom", let go of negative self-talk.

Be proud and enjoy being a housewife.

I am XYZ, And I Don't have Time

Irrespective of which phase of life you are in today, everyone is busy. One day Biswajeet asked his 4-year kid what he is up to. And the reply came – Dad, don't disturb me, I am busy. Do you think he needs to learn time management. Generally, people think if someone is able to get the work done and achieve their goals they have good time management skills. No doubts tools and methods are important to manage time, but here is something which is applicable to everyone under this planet. Carefully read the following two persons' way of presentation.

Jo:

1. No matter how much I try, I am always late.

2. I know this is bad, but I never finish what I start.

3. I don't set any goals because, I have never achieved any.

4. I am too busy to socialize.

5. You don't know how my life situations are, I am too busy to even die.

Mo:

1. I am always on time.

2. When I miss my goal, I change the date, not the goal.

3. No matter how busy I am, I always find time to exercise.

4.   I can complete any task easily.

5.   I know what is important and I always find time to do that and finish it.

Do you see the difference? Who do you think would be a better person at time management? Few people have trained their brains to always talk negatively. I really feel sad when someone boasts about the fact that he or she is super busy. When you say I am always late and people say the same about you, you have created the mental block. Next time even if you try to be on time, the whole world would act against you to be on time. And very aptly you claim that because of the situations I was late today. Stop doing that from this very moment.

"Noone cares how busy you are, no one cares what situations you are going through, and no one can solve your life issues."

So, by reiterating the negative statements you are only complicating your life. The problem is most of the people don't know it's a problem. So next time you say any of the statement spoken by Jo above, stop and change the statement immediately as follows:

1.   I used to be late, but I have figured out how to be on time always.

2.   Whatever I start, I always finish and then only I move to the next.

3.   I have learnt how to set goals and achieve them.

4.   I always find some time to socialize.

5.   My life is pretty much settled, and I am enjoying every moment of it.

Yes, initially, the negative side of your brain would not allow you to speak that. Believe me, once you carefully practice doing this, you not only would feel better, but you would start to manage time effectively and enjoy life.

Self-talk – the easiest solution to any problem

Negative self-talk can significantly undermine self-confidence, especially in areas where we feel insecure or uncertain. When we constantly criticize ourselves or focus on our perceived shortcomings, it creates a cycle of self-doubt that holds us back from realizing our full potential. This inner dialogue not only diminishes our belief in our abilities but also contributes to feelings of helplessness and inadequacy. Over time, this lack of confidence can make us avoid challenges and prevent us from taking risks, ultimately limiting our growth and success.

Building self-confidence through positive self-talk is an ongoing practice that requires patience and consistency. As we change the way we speak to ourselves, we begin to view challenges and setbacks as opportunities for learning rather than threats. This shift in perspective allows us to approach tasks with greater resilience, determination, and a sense of self-assurance. The more we practice positive self-talk, the stronger our belief in our own abilities becomes, and this newfound confidence empowers us to take on bigger goals and achieve greater results.

Conclusion

Imagine there is a bank that credits your account each morning with ₹86,400.

It carries over no balance from day to day. Every evening the bank deletes whatever part of the balance you failed to use during the day.

What would you do? Draw out every cent, of course!!!

Each of us has such a bank. Its name is TIME.

Every morning, it credits you with 86,400 seconds.

Every night it writes off, as lost, whatever of this you have failed to invest to good purpose.

It carries over no balance. It allows no overdraft.

Each day it opens a new account for you.

Each night it burns the remains of the day.

If you fail to use the day's deposits, the loss is yours.

There is no going back. There is no drawing against the "tomorrow".

You must live in the present on today's deposits.

Invest it so as to get from it the utmost in health, happiness, and success!

The clock is running. Make the most of today.

To realize the value of ONE YEAR, ask a student who failed a grade.

To realize the value of ONE MONTH, ask a mother who gave birth to a premature baby.

To realize the value of ONE WEEK, ask the editor of a weekly newspaper.

To realize the value of ONE HOUR, ask the lovers who are waiting to meet.

To realize the value of ONE MINUTE, ask a person who missed the train.

To realize the value of ONE SECOND, ask a person who just avoided an accident.

Treasure every moment that you have! And reassure it more because you shared it with someone special, special enough to spend your time.

Remember that time waits for no one.

Yesterday is history. Tomorrow is mystery. Today is a gift.

That's why it's called the present!

"Time is not something to be conquered or controlled, but something to be respected and used wisely."

Have Some Fun with TIME

"Time is a great teacher, but unfortunately it kills all its pupils."

– Louis Hector Berlioz

"I am extraordinarily patient, provided I get my own way in the end."

– Margaret Thatcher

"The bad news is time flies. The good news is you're the pilot."

– Michael Altshuler

"Time is what we want most, but what we use worst."

– William Penn

"Don't watch the clock; do what it does. Keep going."

– Sam Levenson (Though not exactly funny, this can be humorous in a sarcastic context.)

"I have a very bad habit of procrastinating. I'm so good at it that I can get a task done at the last minute. right after it was supposed to be done!"

–Unknown

"Time management is the art of making you feel guilty about all the things you didn't do."

– Unknown

"Procrastination is the art of keeping up with yesterday."

– Don Marquis

"I love deadlines. I love the whooshing sound they make as they fly by."

– Douglas Adams

"If you think time flies, try missing a plane."

– Unknown

"Time is money, unless you're a student. Then, time is a nap."

– Unknown

"I'm on a seafood diet. I see food and I eat it... but I'm still working on my time management."

– Unknown

"My life feels like a test I didn't study for."

– Unknown

"Time is like a river. You can't touch the same water twice, because the flow that has passed will never pass again."

– Unknown (But let's be honest, it's a lot easier to touch the snooze button multiple times!)

"I always arrive late at the office, but I make up for it by leaving early."

– Charles Lamb

"I don't have a time management problem. I have a 'I'm-too-busy-being-awesome' problem."

– Unknown

"Time management is just planning your procrastination."

– Unknown

"I'm not procrastinating, I'm doing 'intensive' thinking about the task at hand."

– Unknown

"I swear, time just speeds up the older I get. Or maybe it's just my ability to organize it that's slowing down."

– Unknown

"Time management is the key to success. unless you're a nap enthusiast."

– Unknown

Get in touch and send the Authors your reviews:

Biswajeet Senapati

Phone: +91-9343834910

Email ID: biswajeet.senapati@gmail.com

YouTube: https://www.youtube.com/c/BiswajeetsStudio

LinkedIn: https://www.linkedin.com/in/biswajeetsenapati/

Facebook: https://www.facebook.com/biswajeet.senapati.3

Dr. Sharda Acharya

Phone: +91-8298877356

Email ID: sharda.acharya2023@gmail.com

LinkedIn: https://www.linkedin.com/in/sharda-acharya-298714267/

To know more check out:

www.biswajeetsenapati.com

Thank You!